"Glory to God in the highest, and on earth peace, good will toward men."

Luke 2:14

CHRISTIAN CHRISTMAS COLORING BOOK

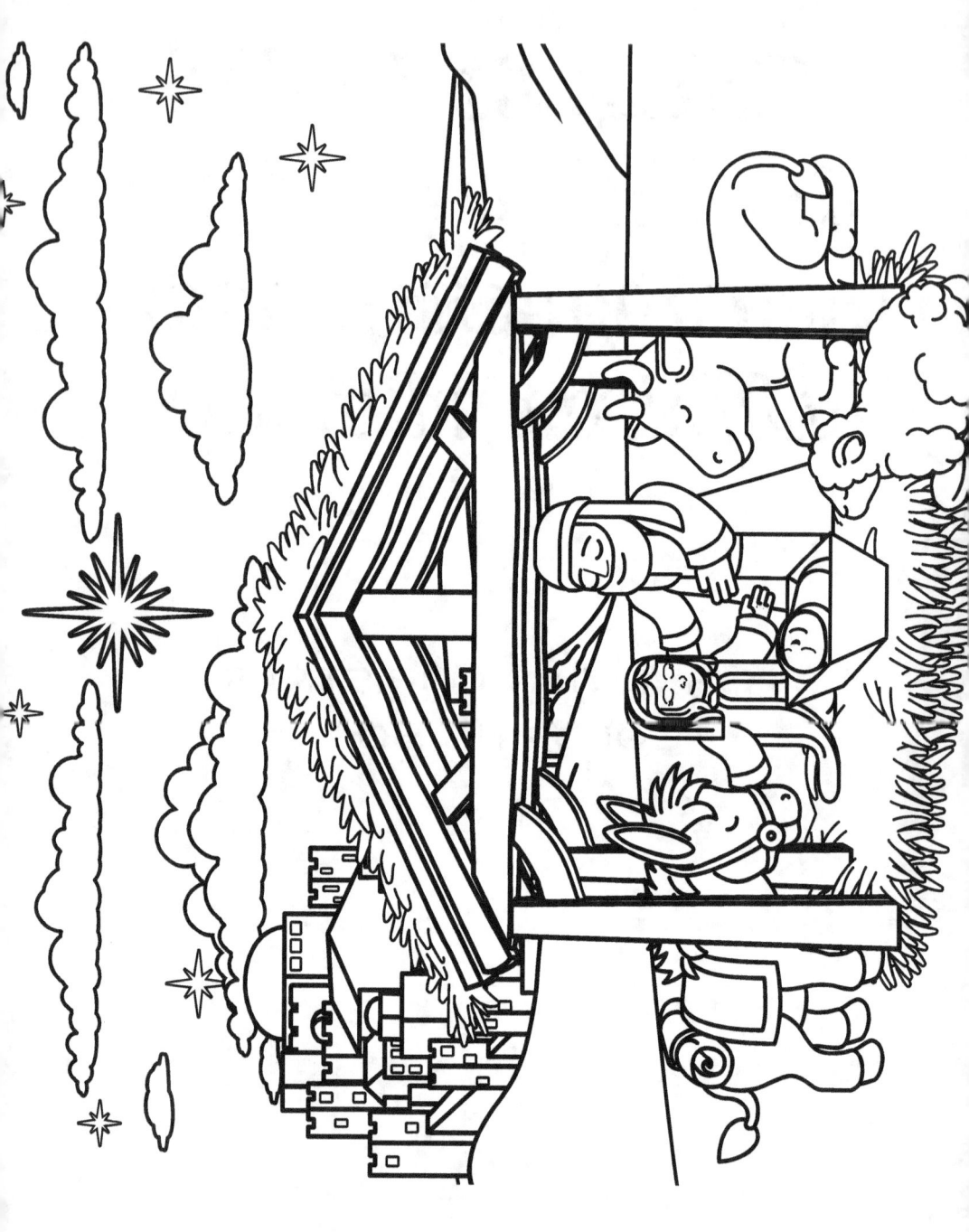

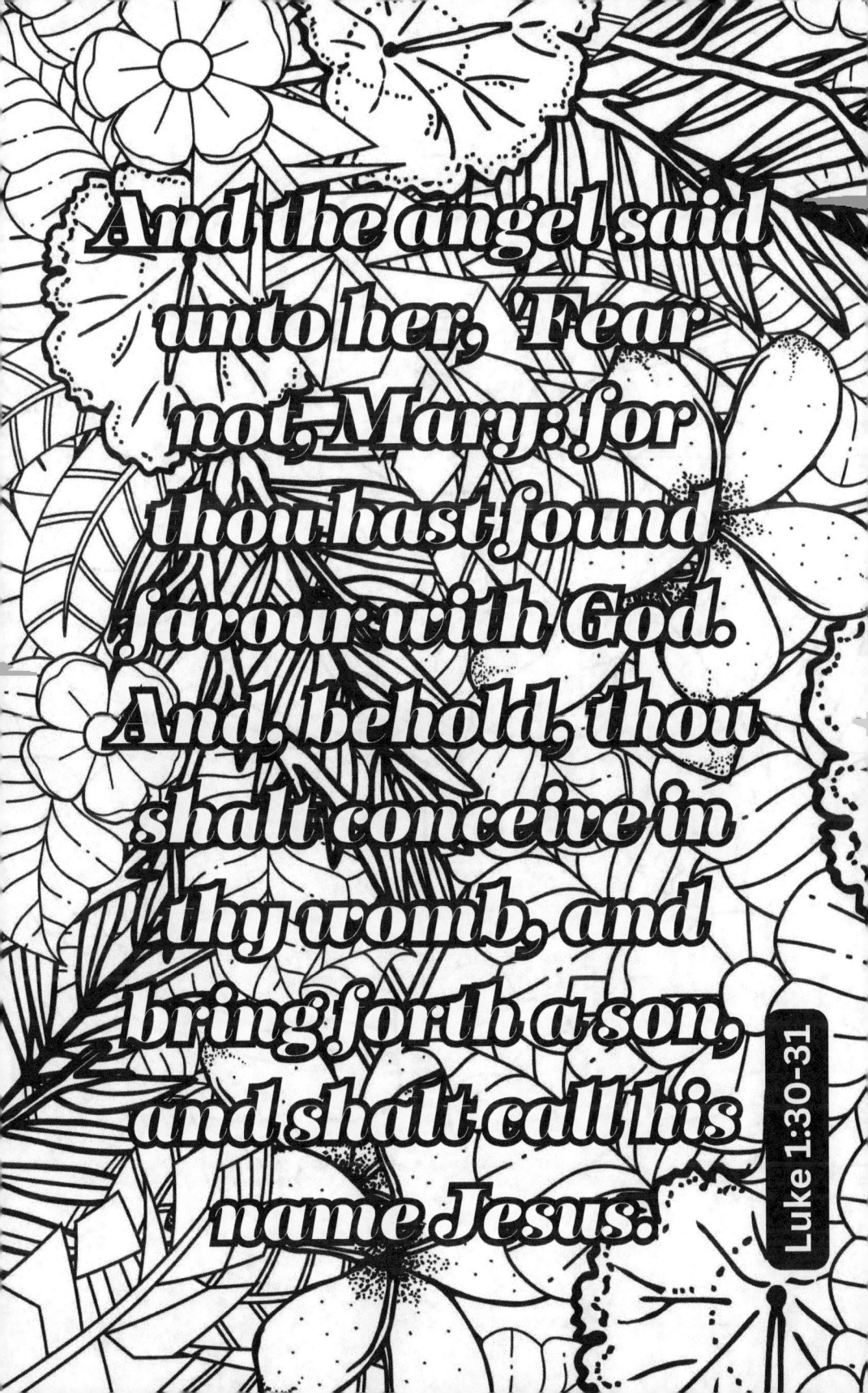

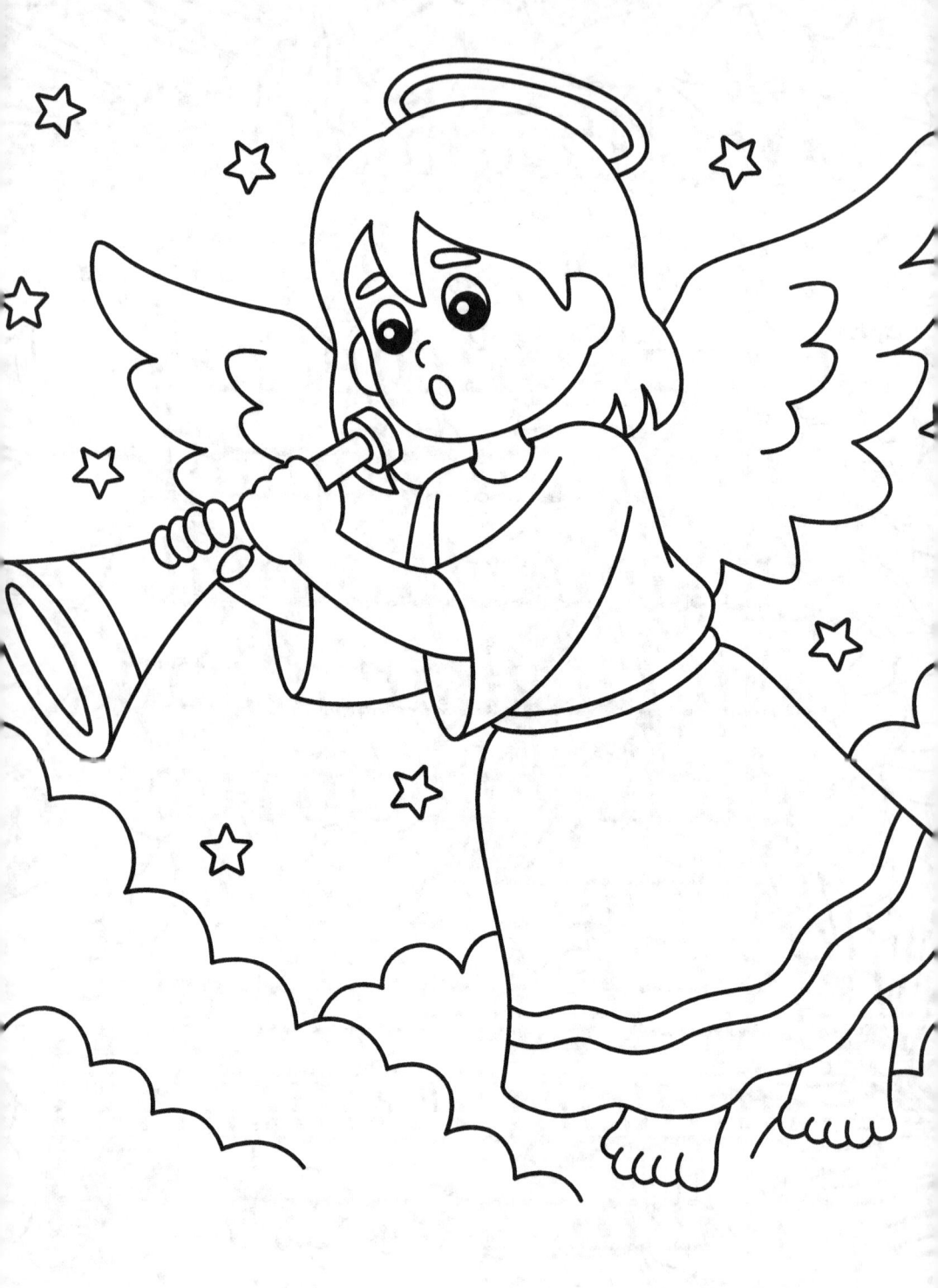

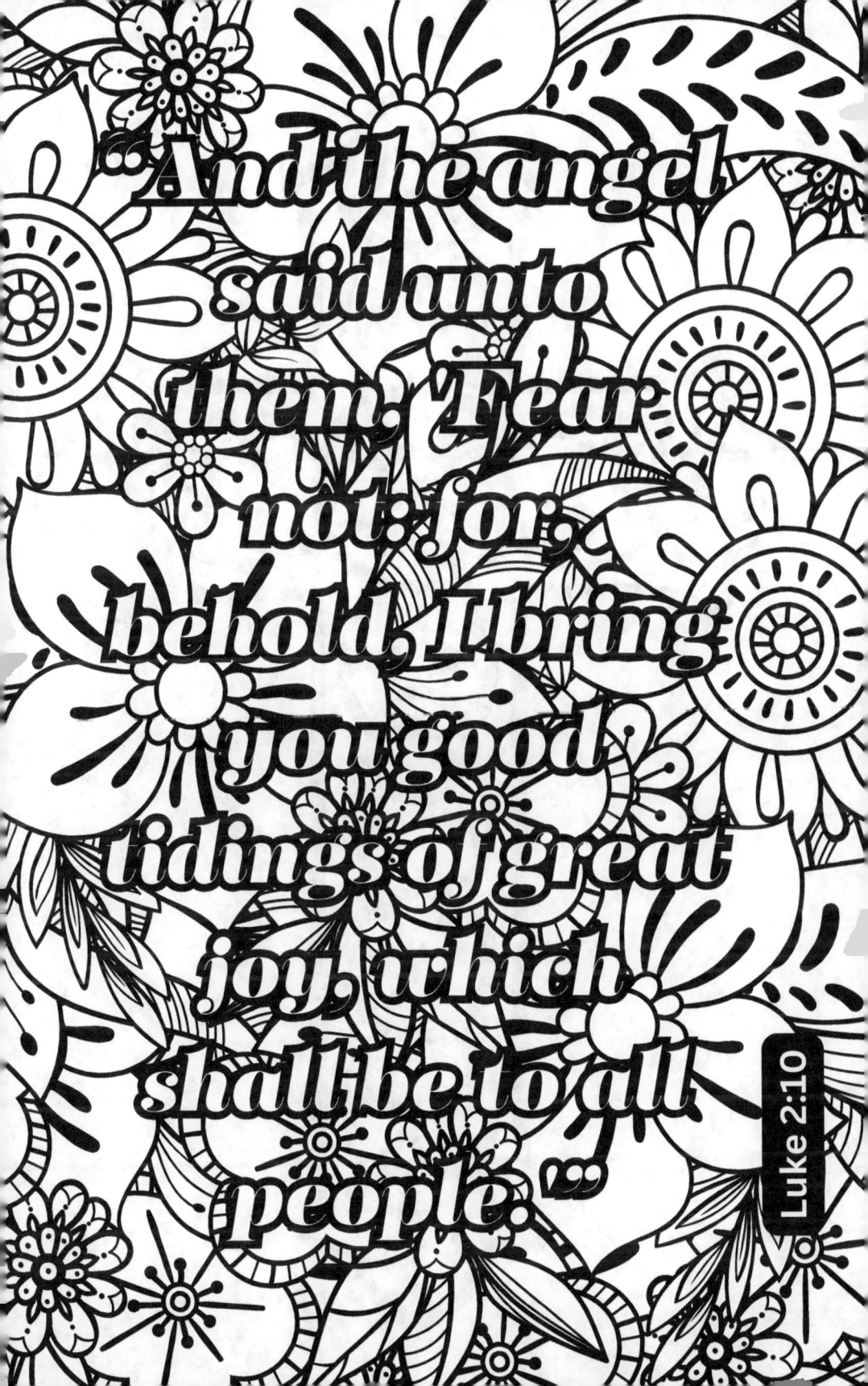

"And the angel said unto them: Fear not: for behold, I bring you good tidings of great joy, which shall be to all people."

Luke 2:10

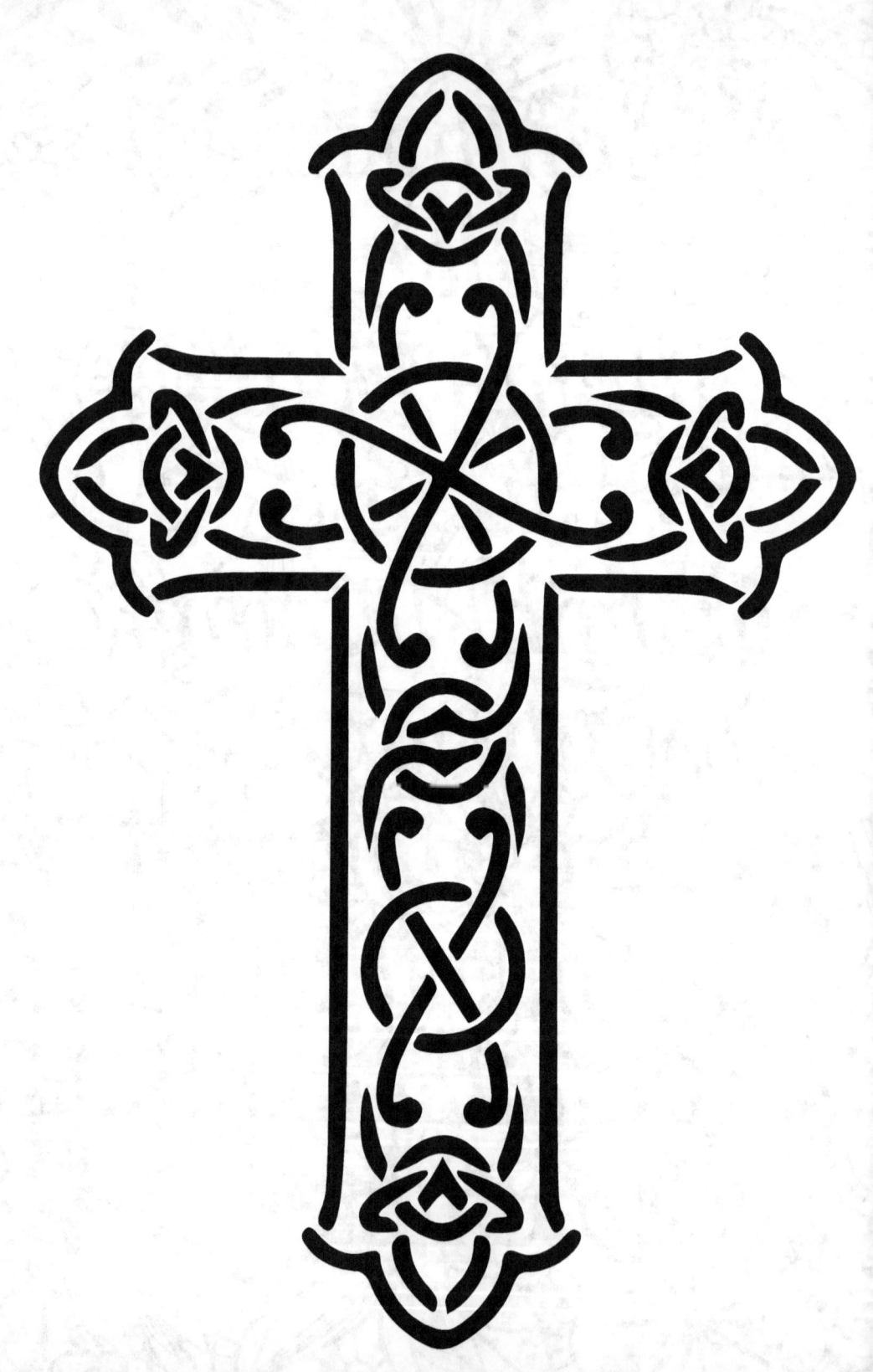

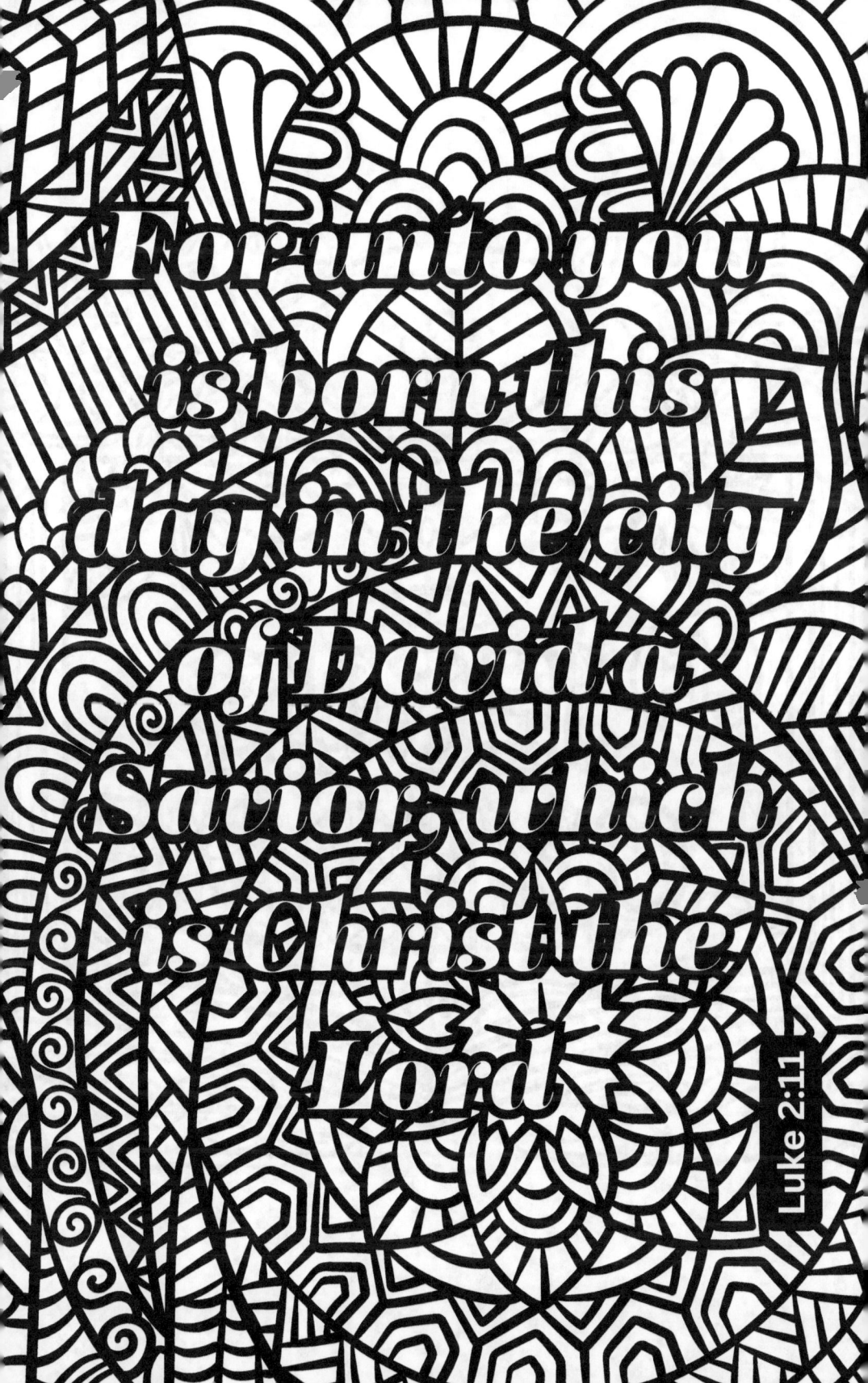

For unto you is born this day in the city of David a Savior, which is Christ the Lord

Luke 2:11

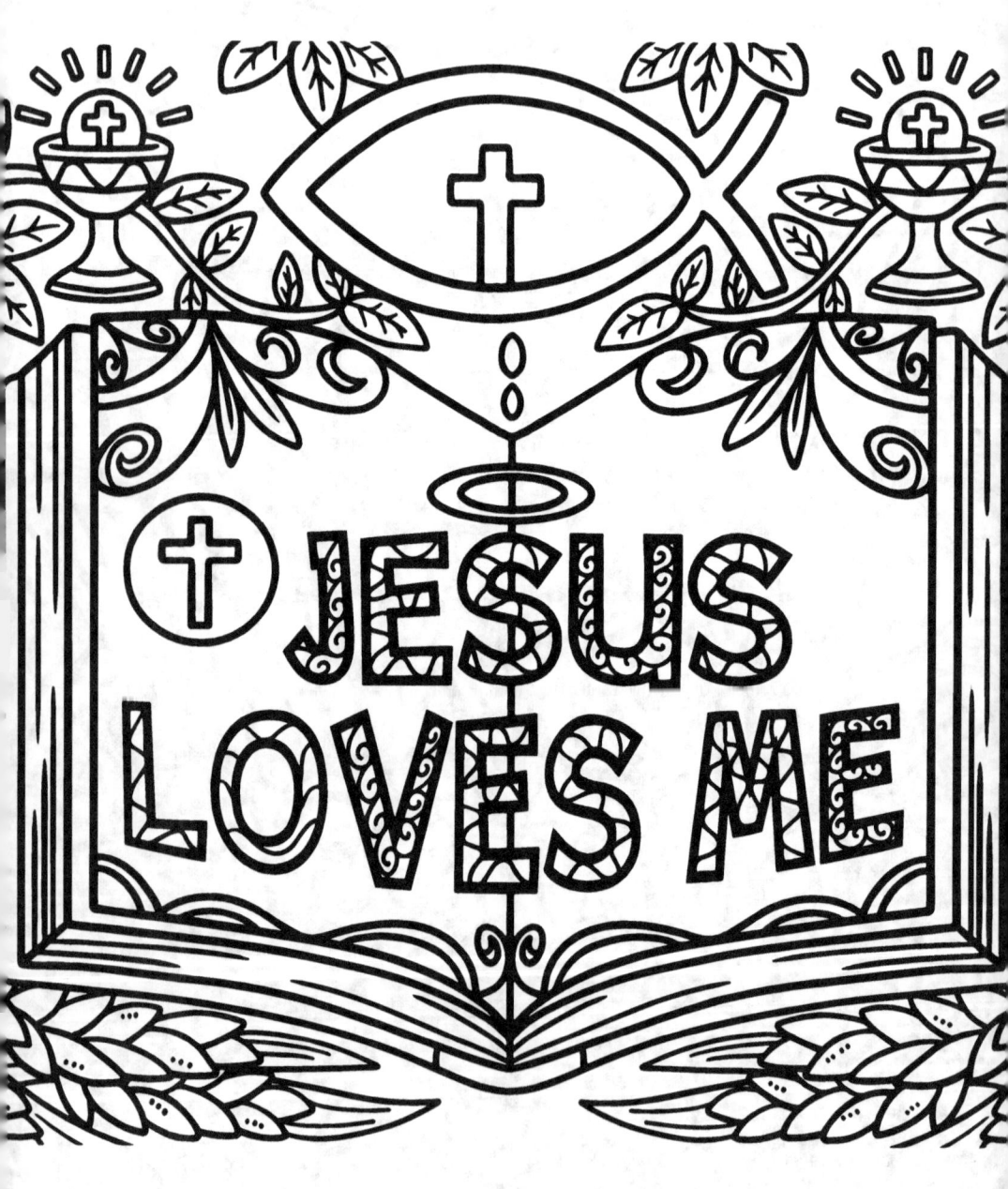

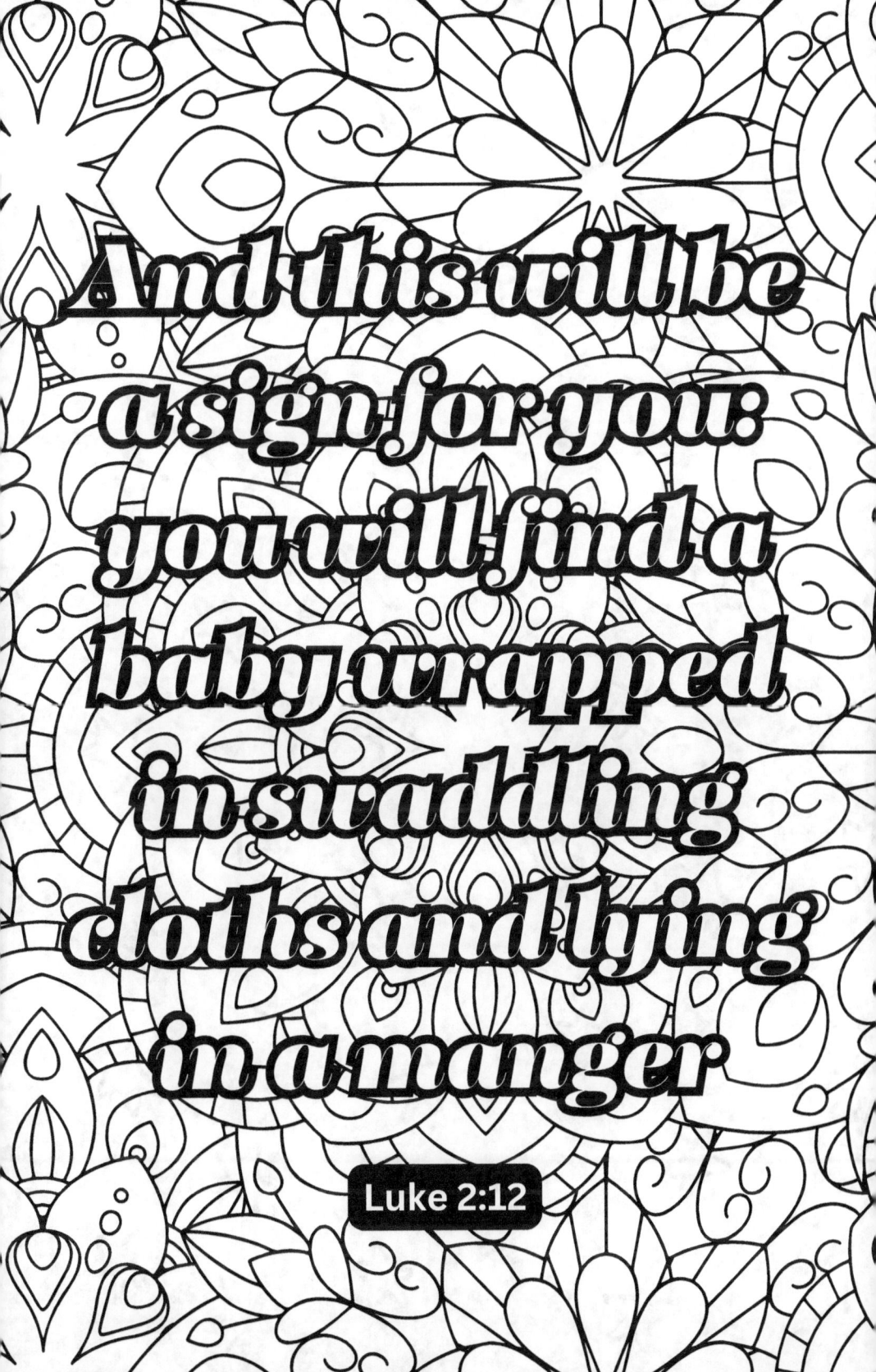

And this will be a sign for you: you will find a baby wrapped in swaddling cloths and lying in a manger

Luke 2:12

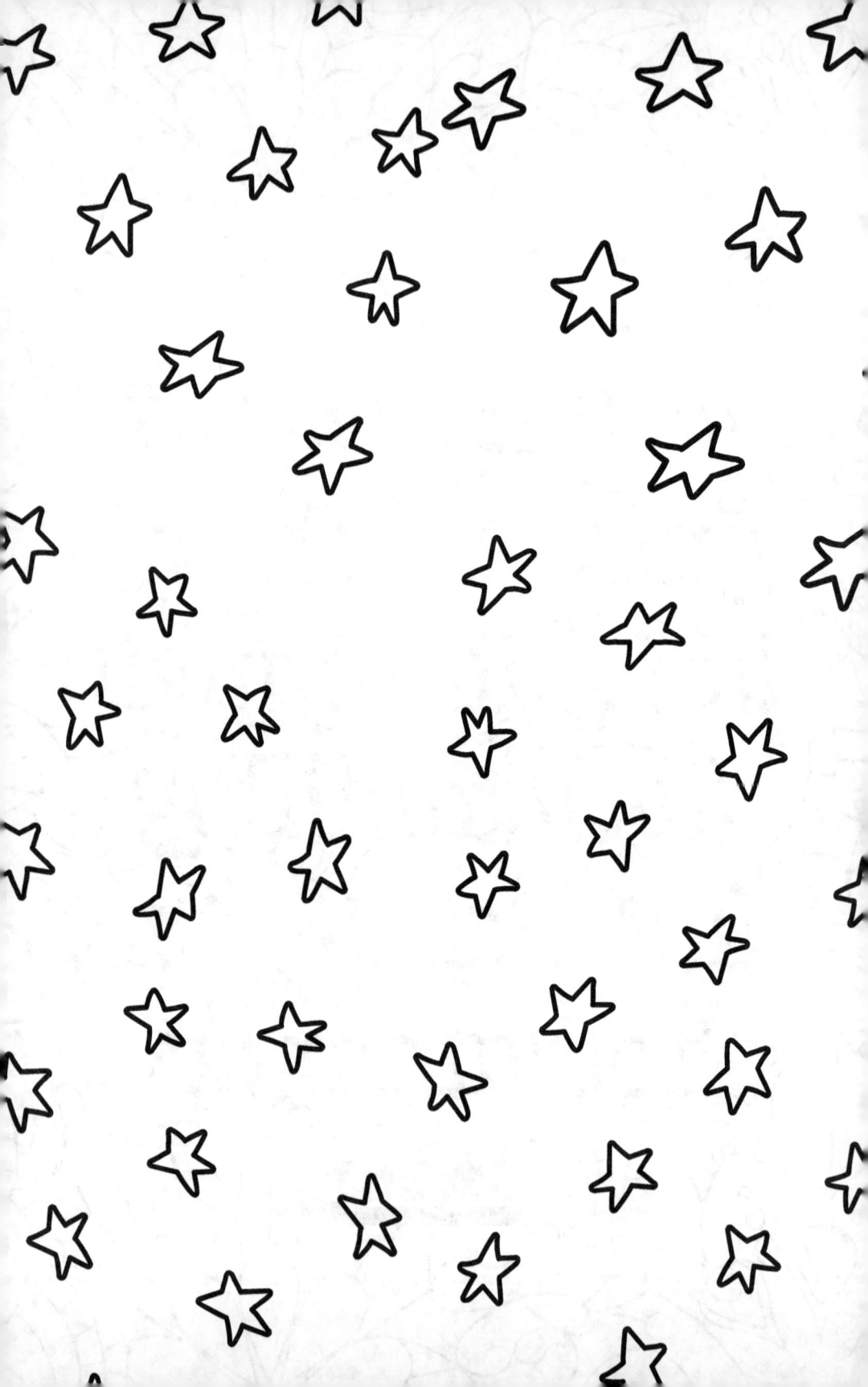

Come, let us greatly rejoice in the Lord; Let us shout aloud to God our savior

Psalm 94:1

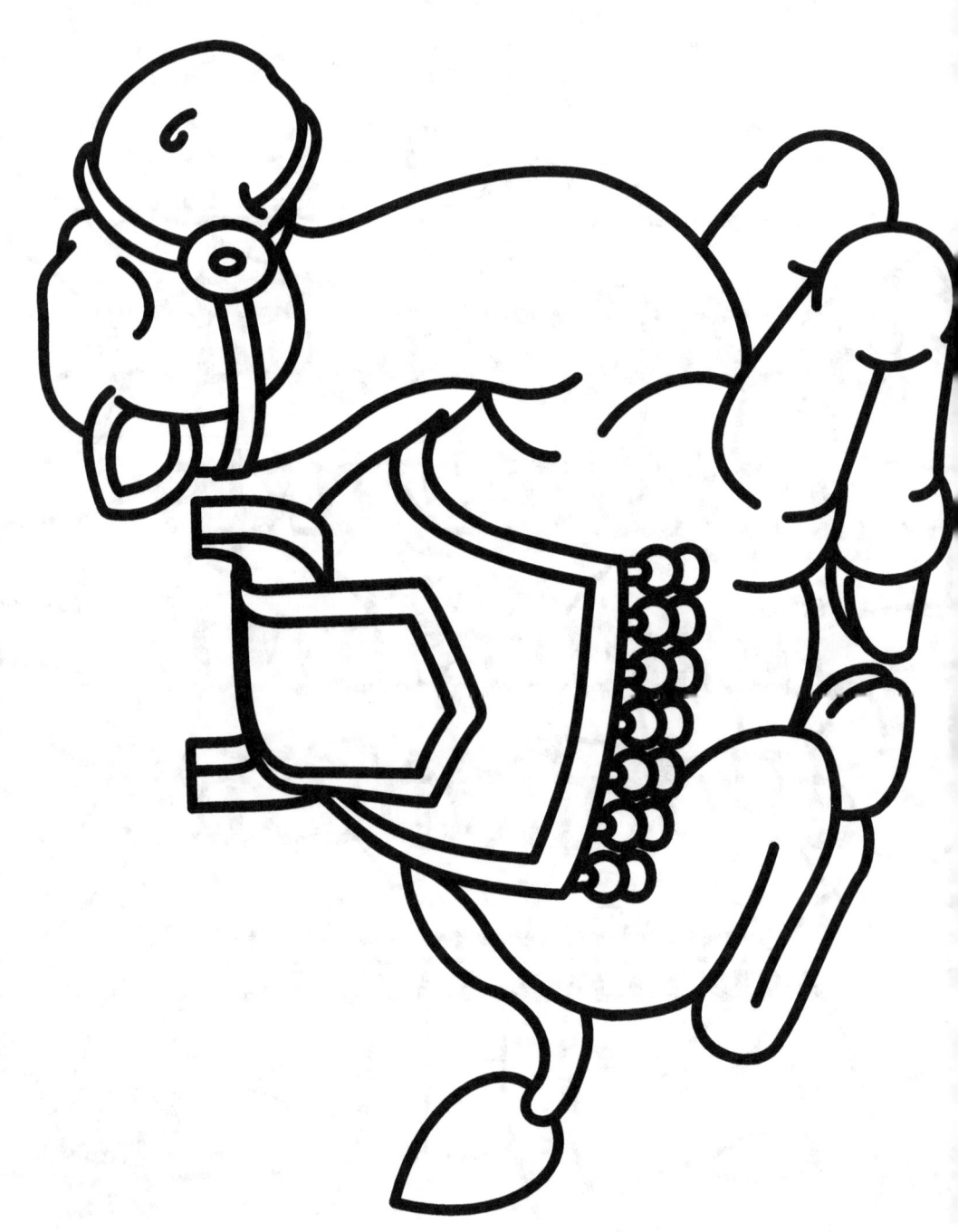

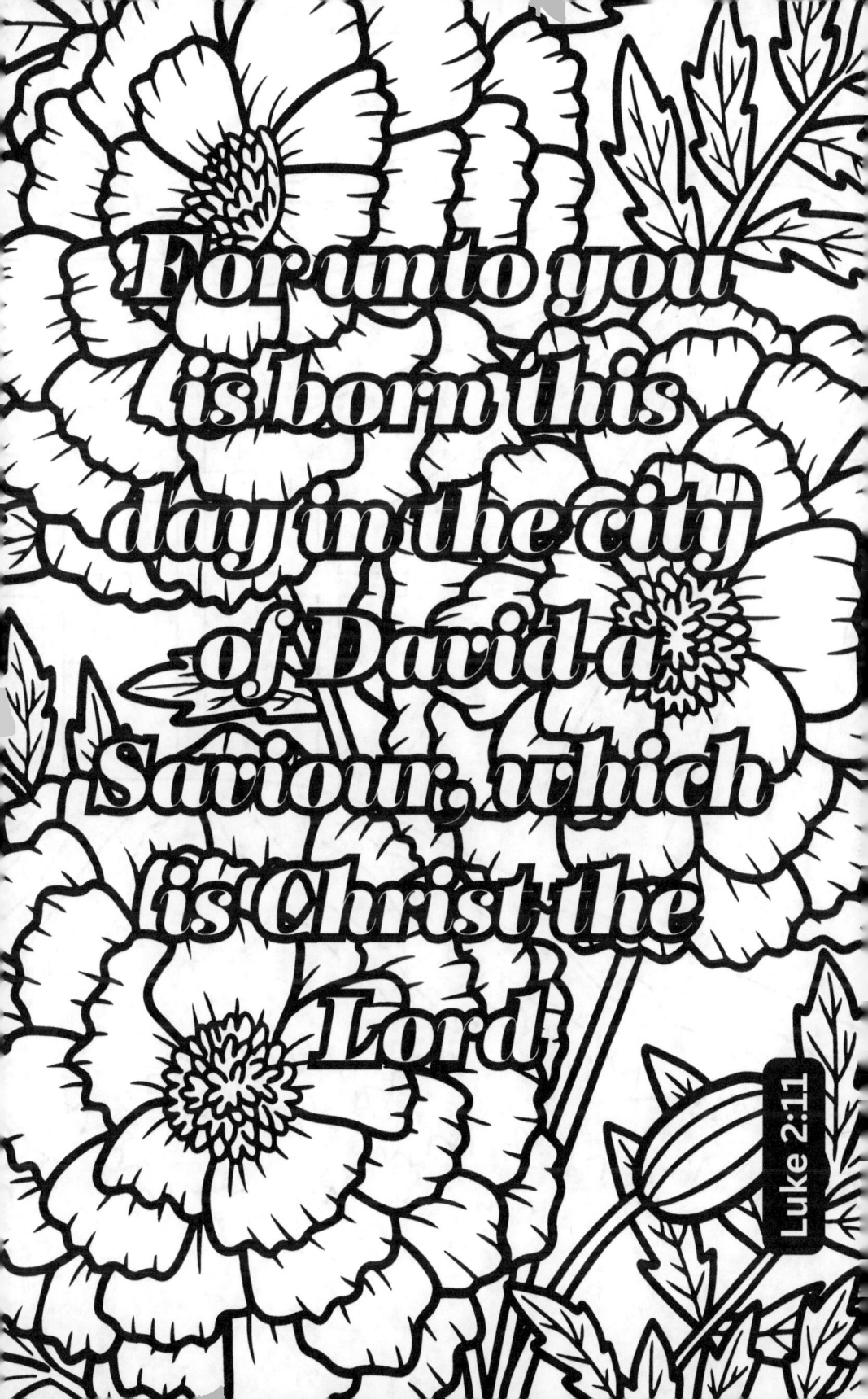

For unto you is born this day in the city of David a Saviour, which is Christ the Lord.

Luke 2:11

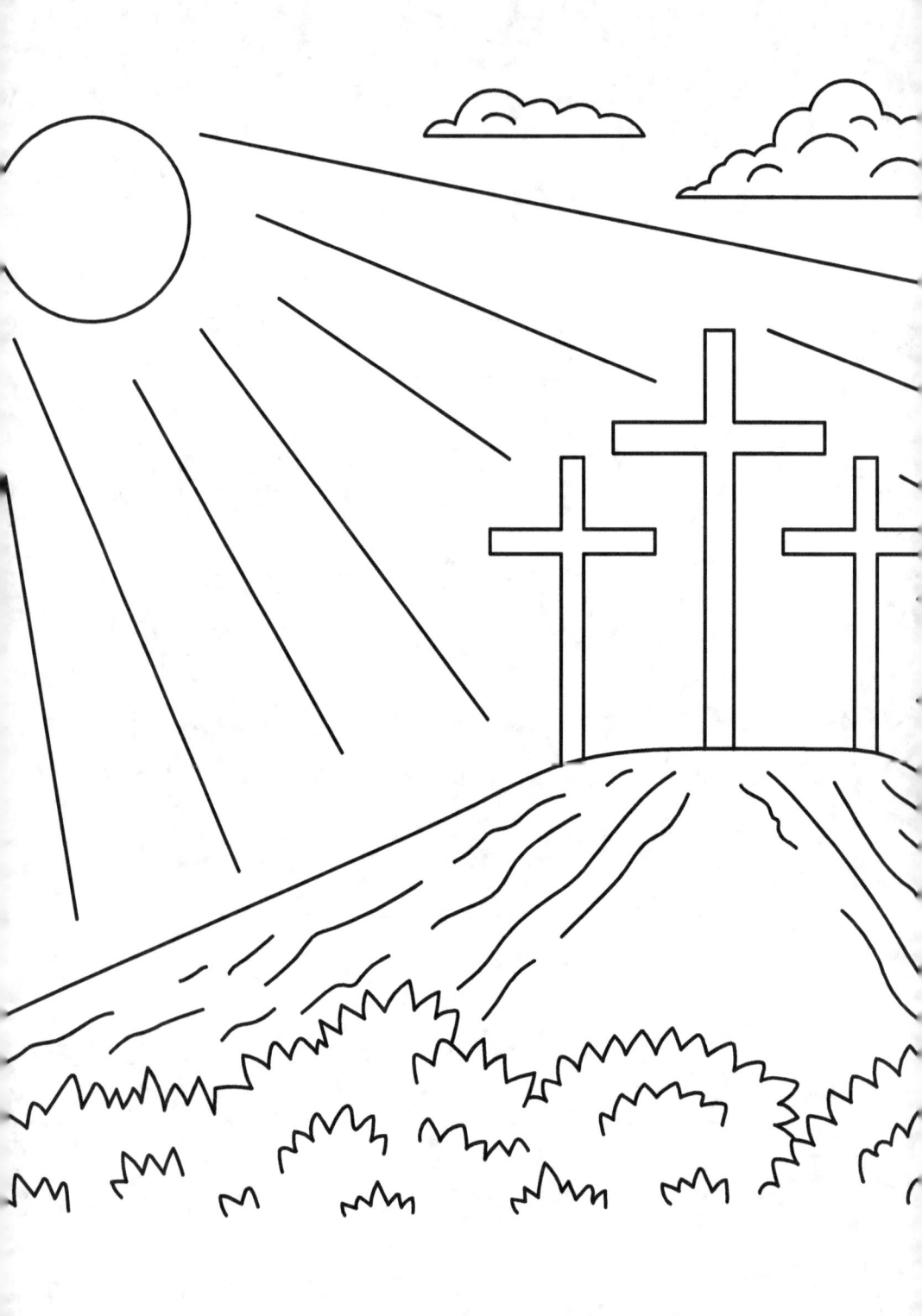

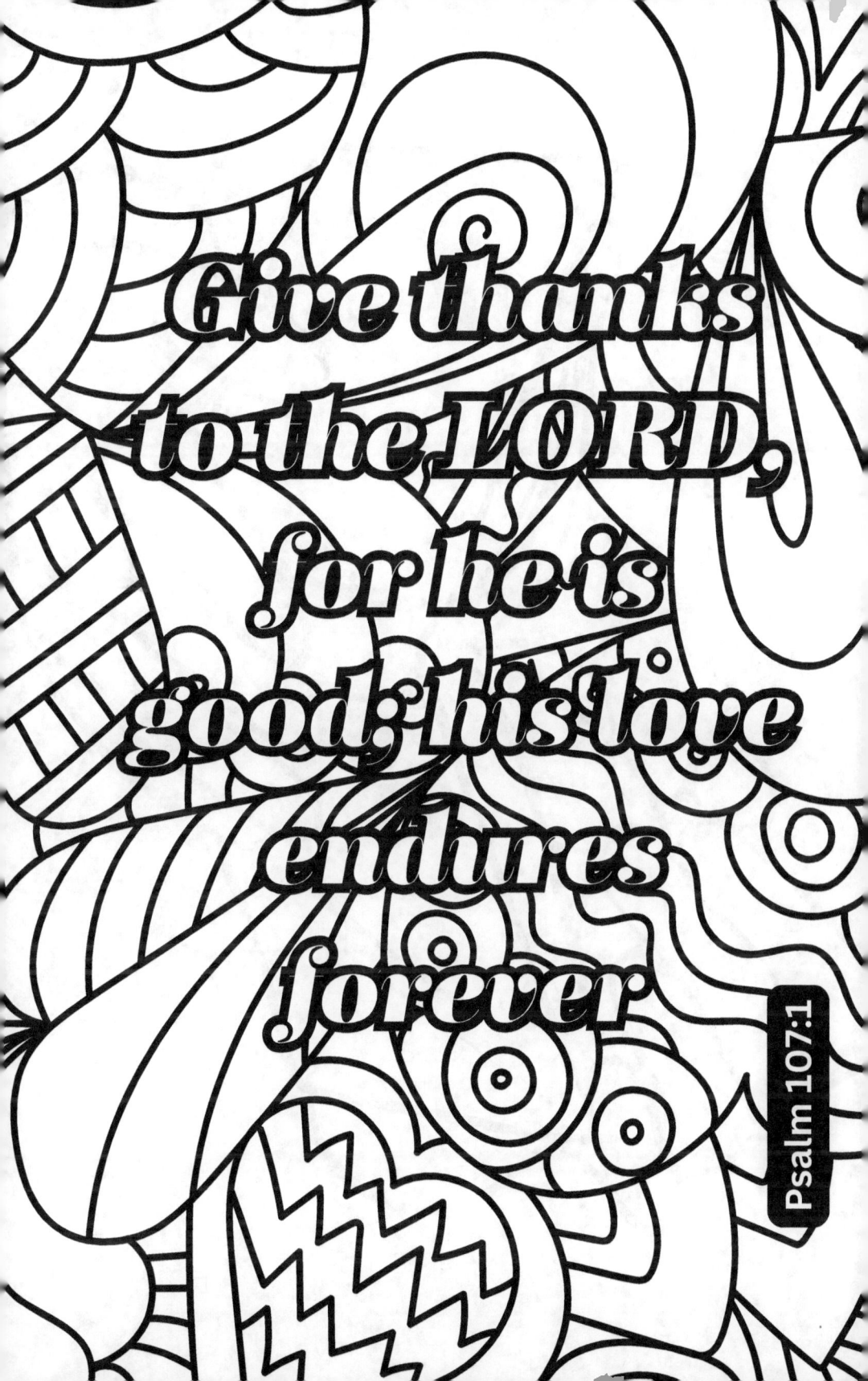

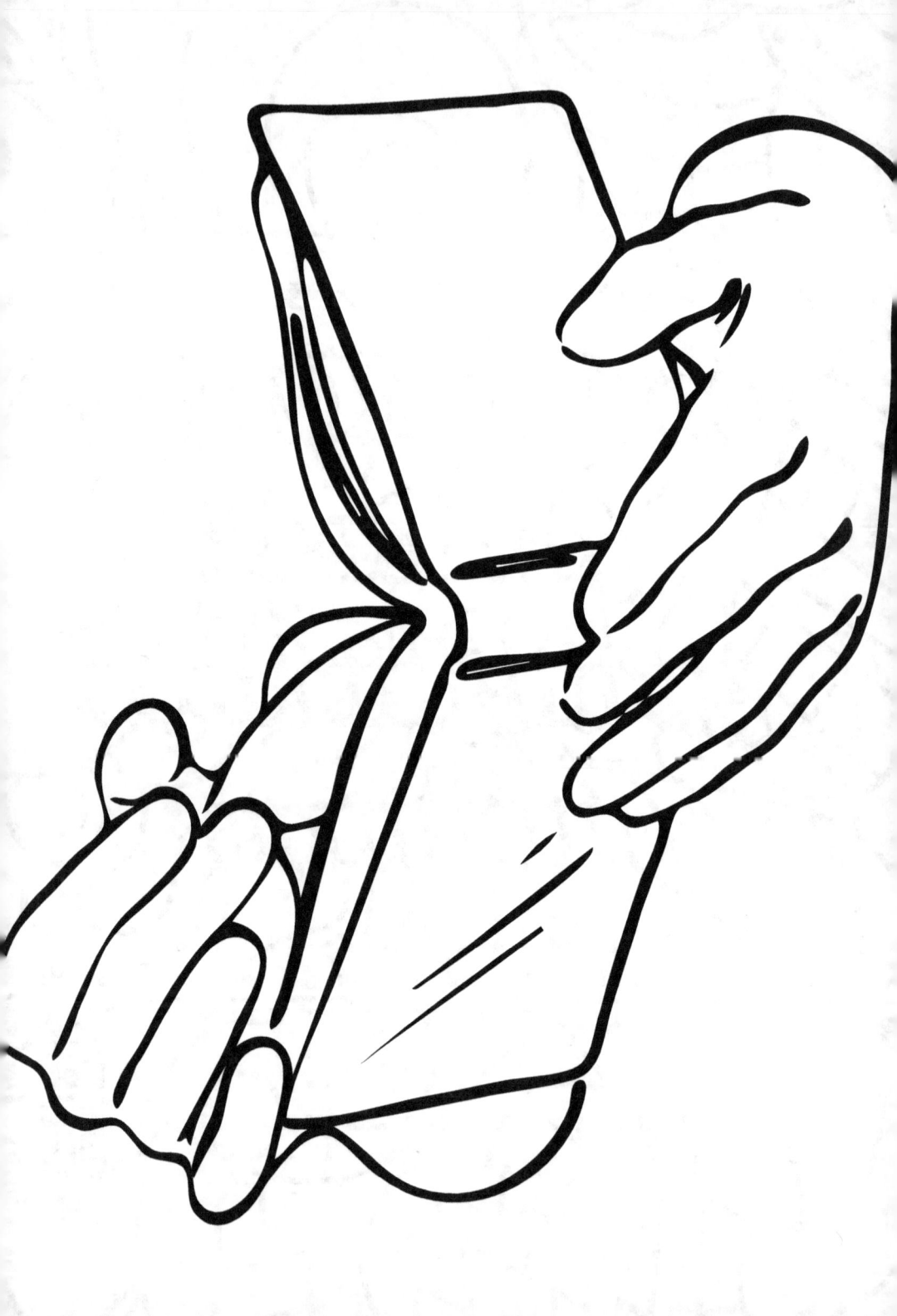

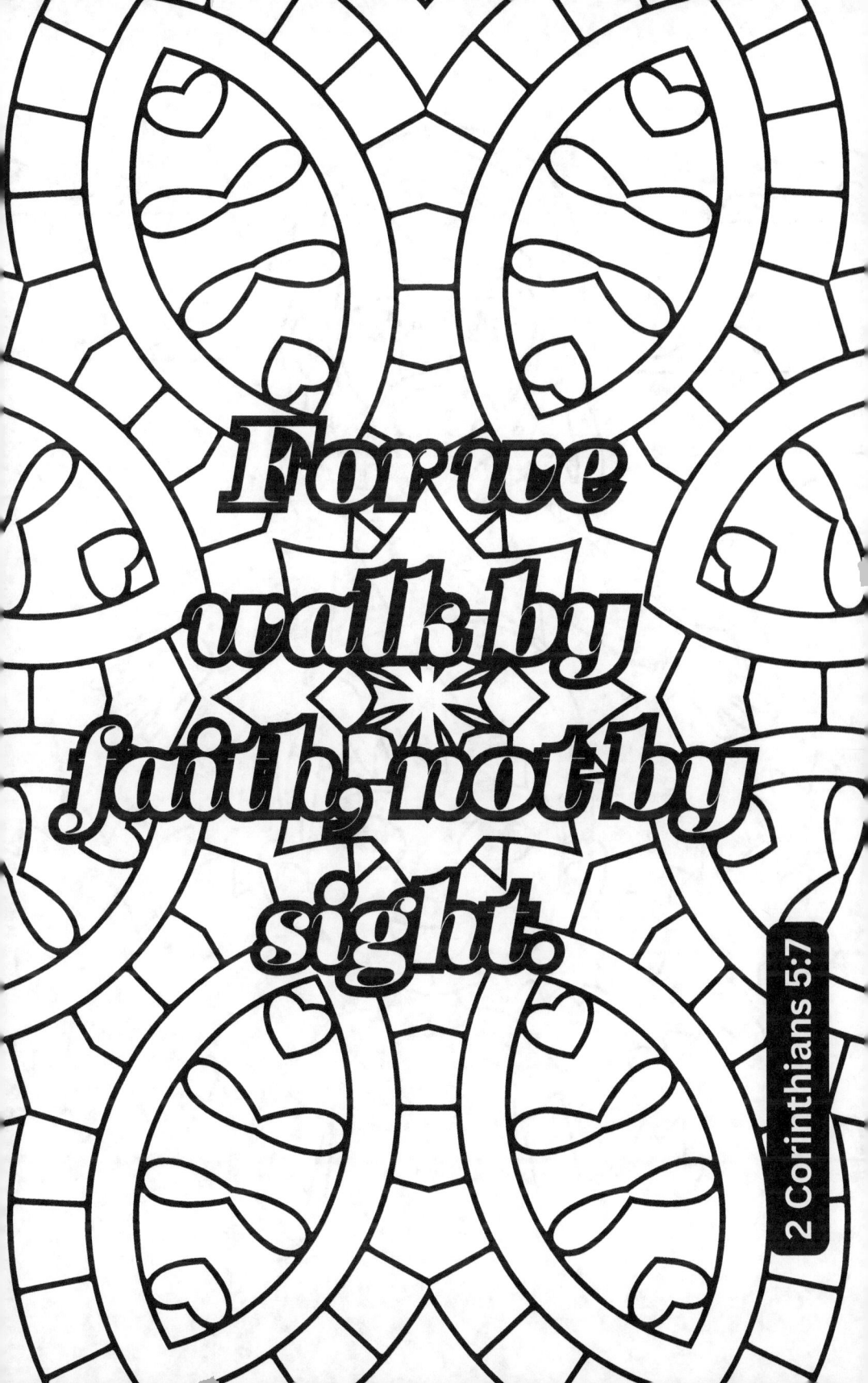

For we walk by faith, not by sight.

2 Corinthians 5:7

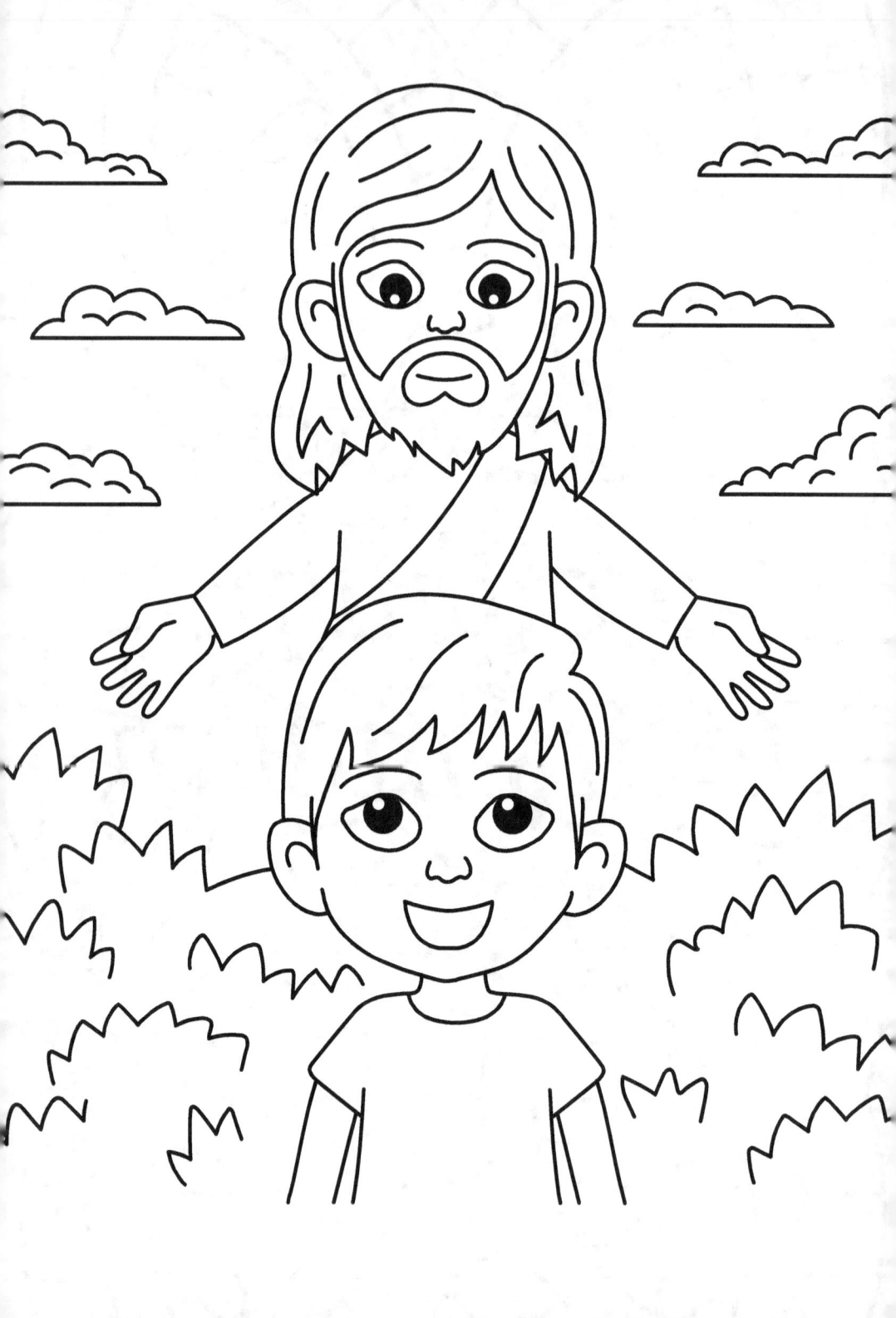

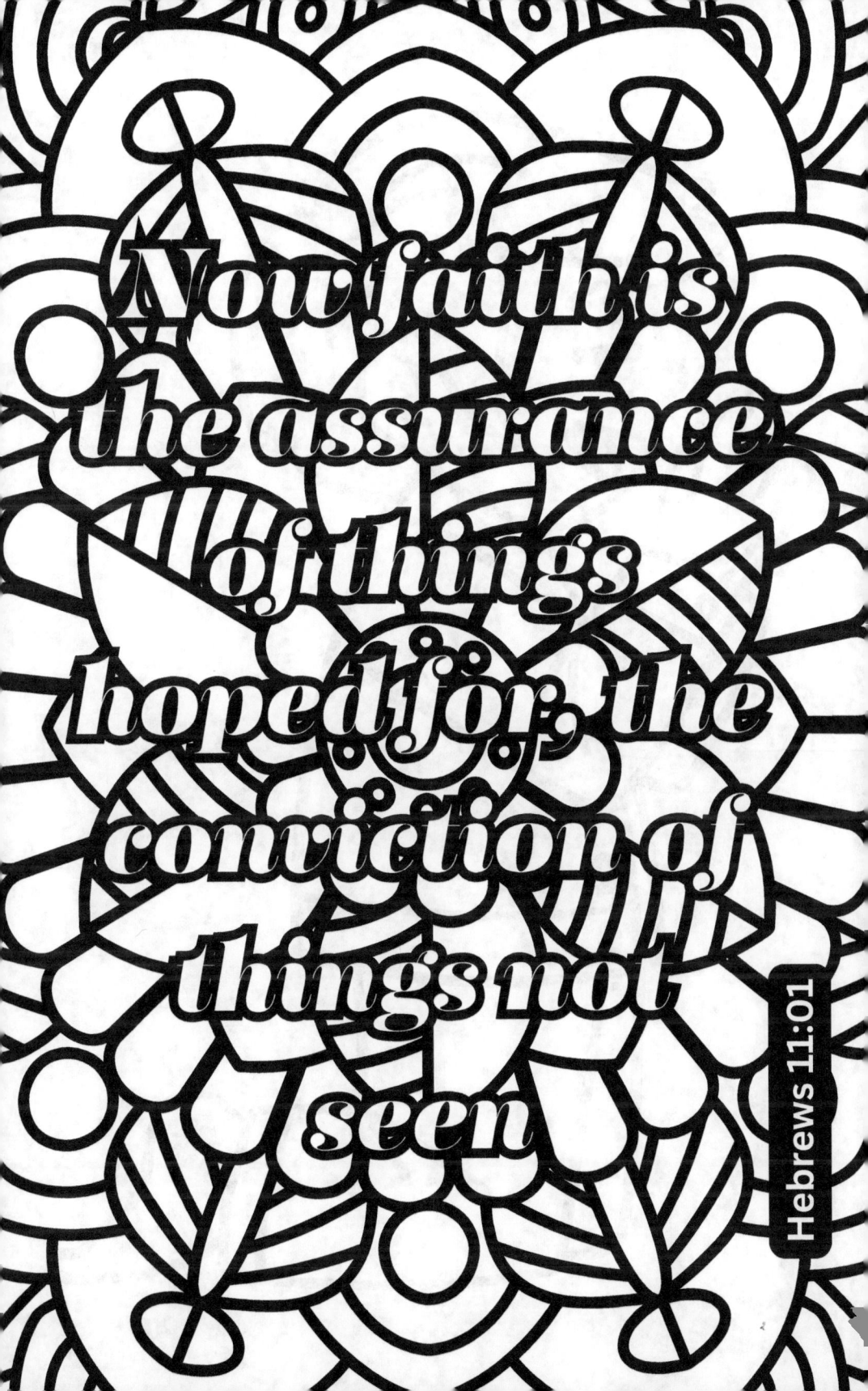

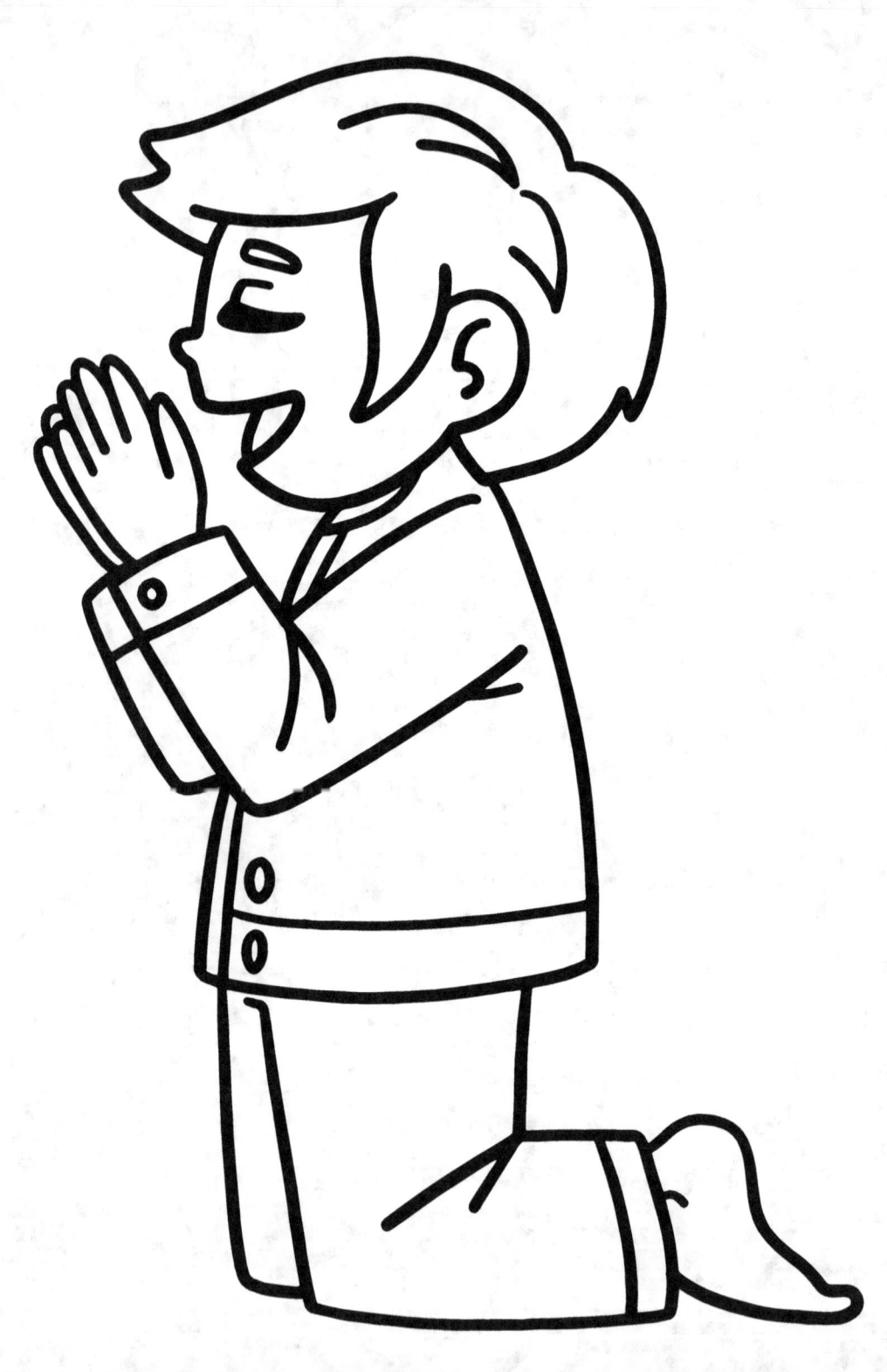

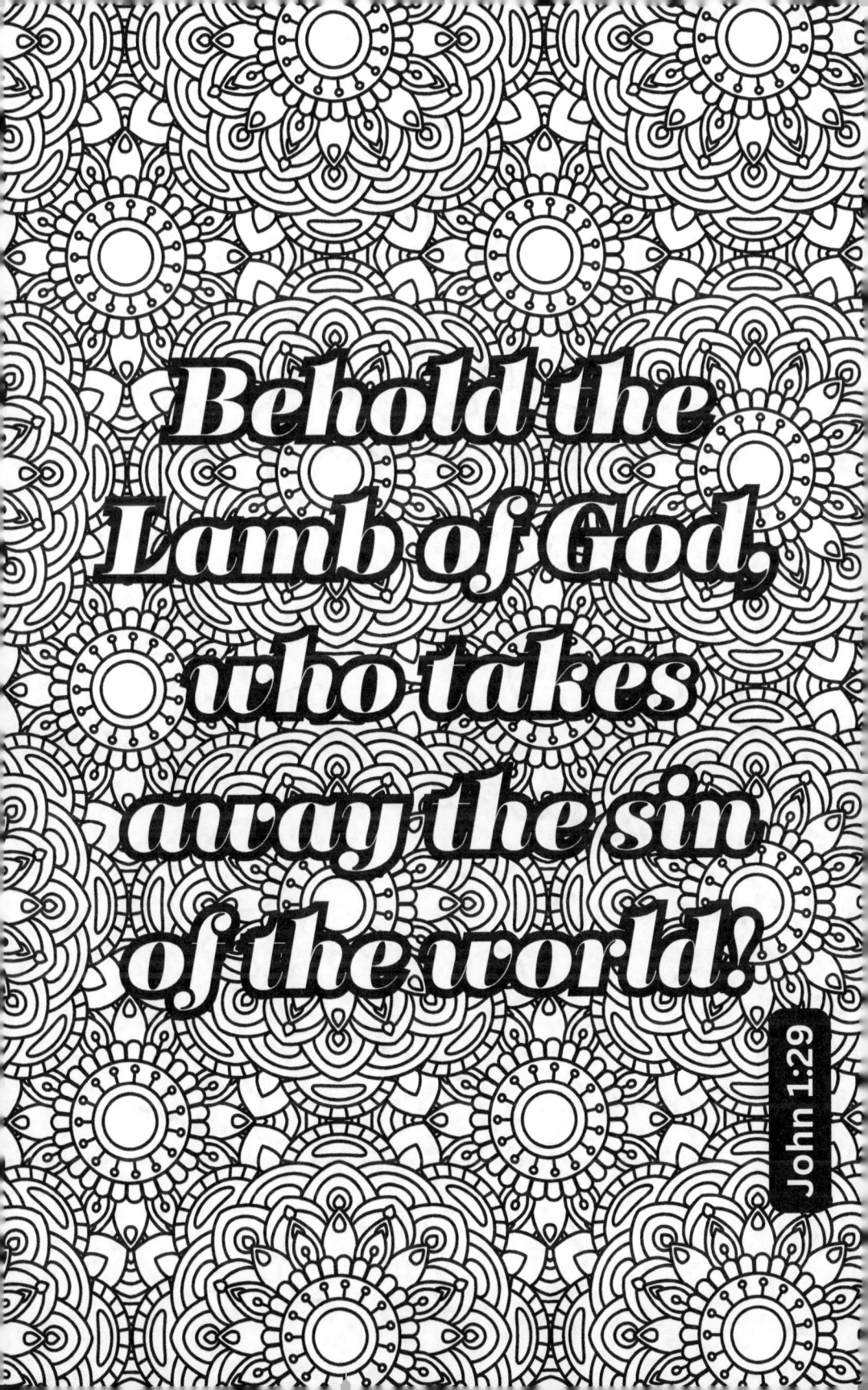

Behold the Lamb of God, who takes away the sin of the world!

John 1:29

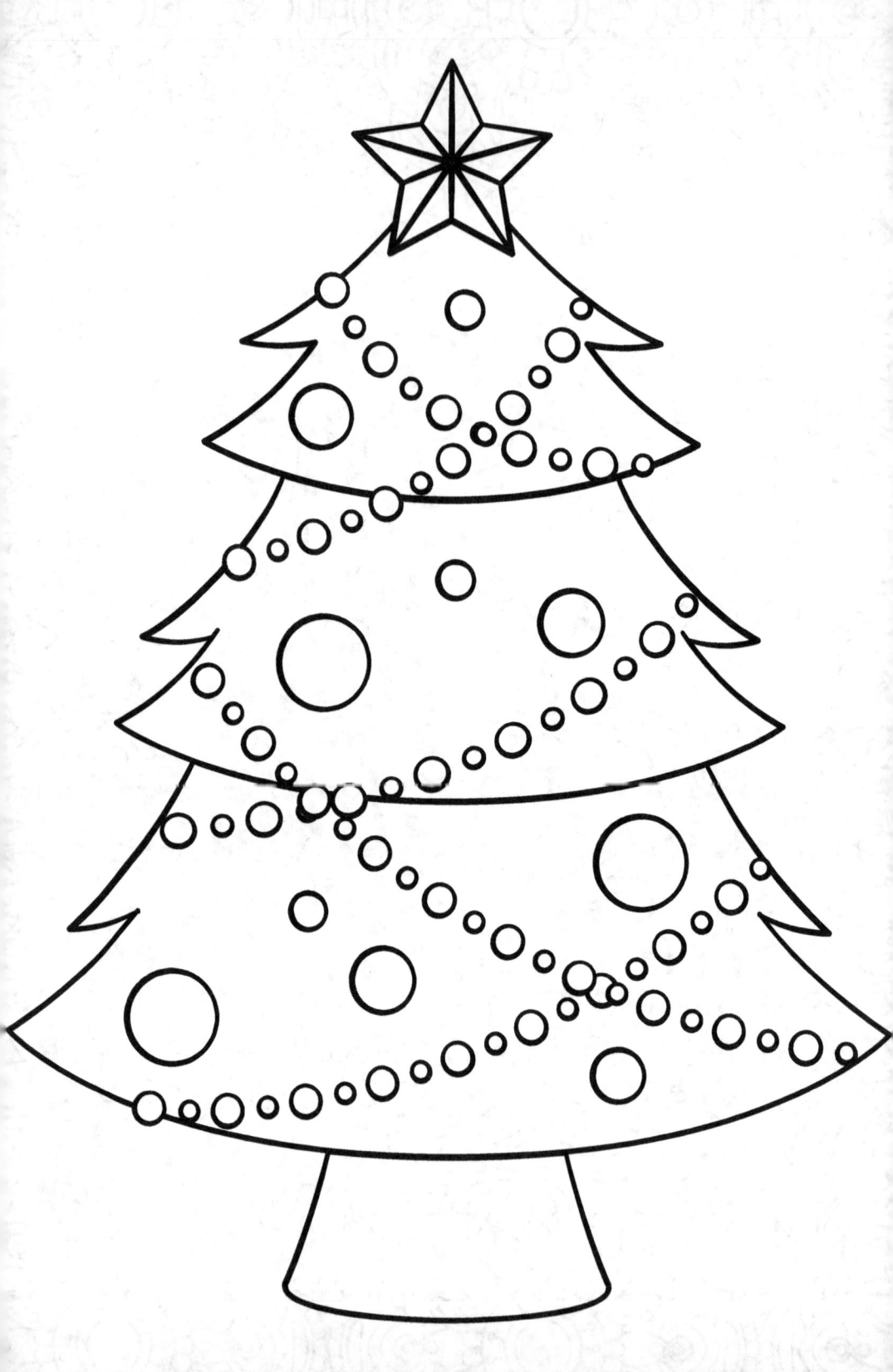

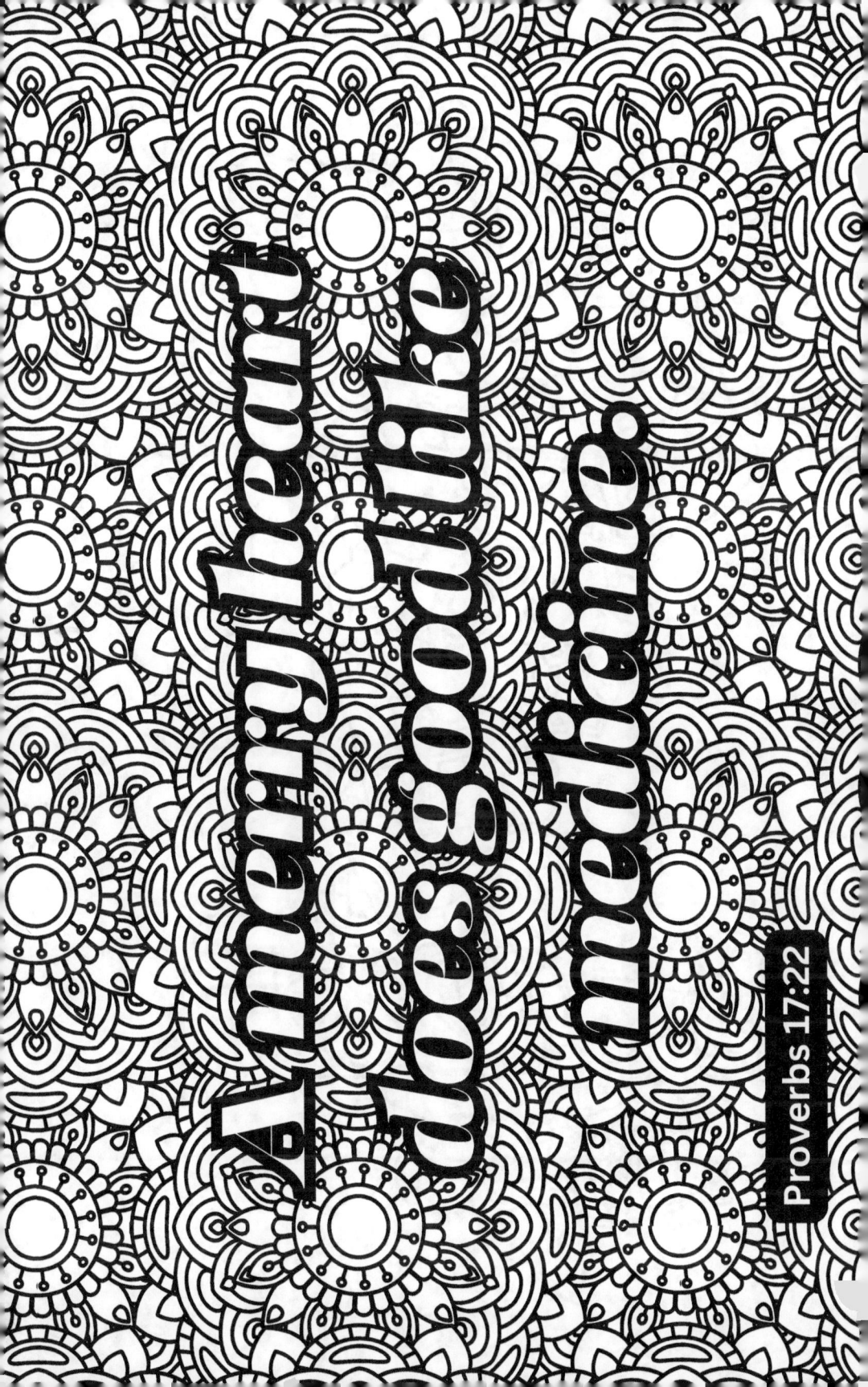

A merry heart does good like medicine.

Proverbs 17:22

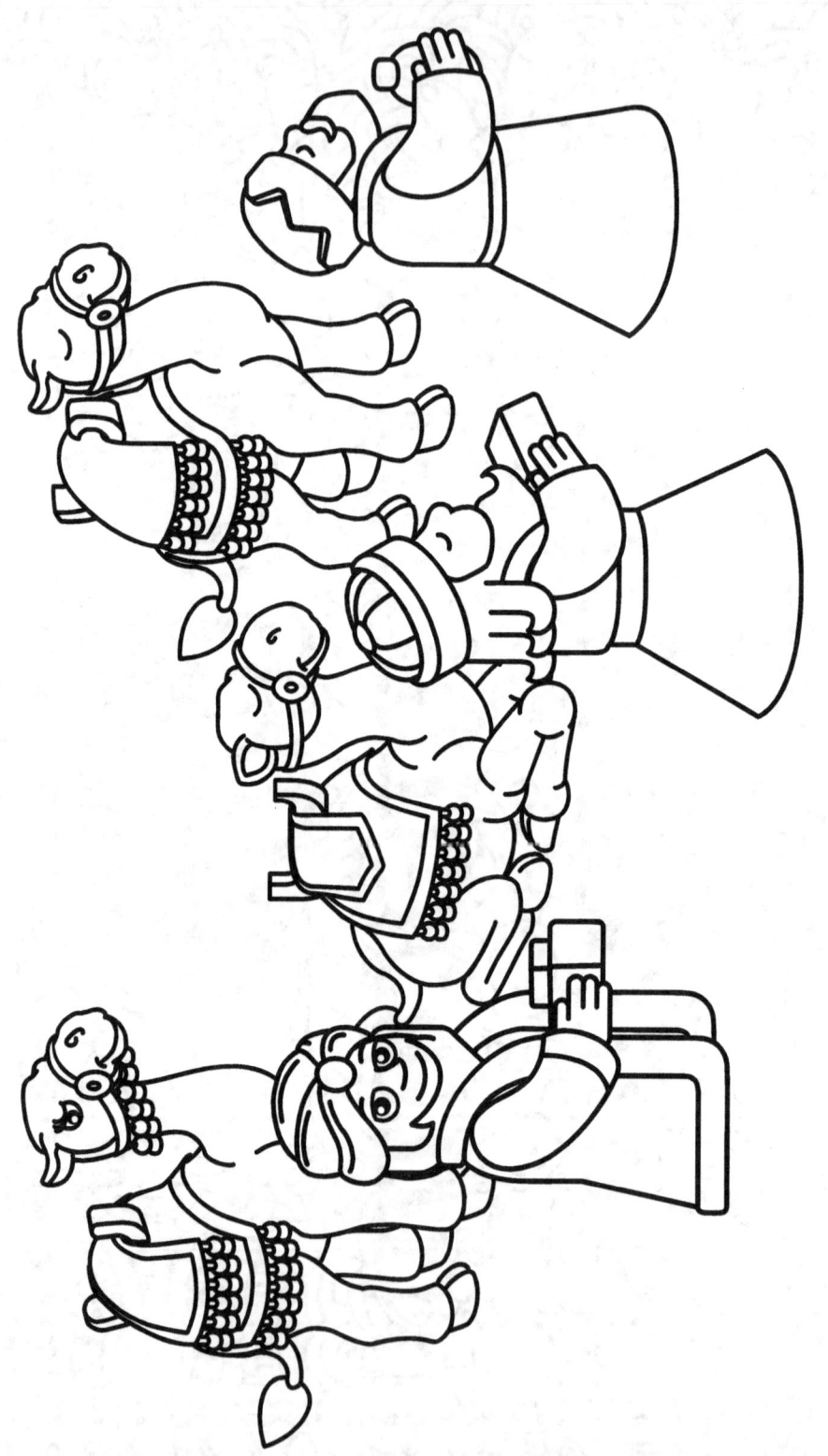

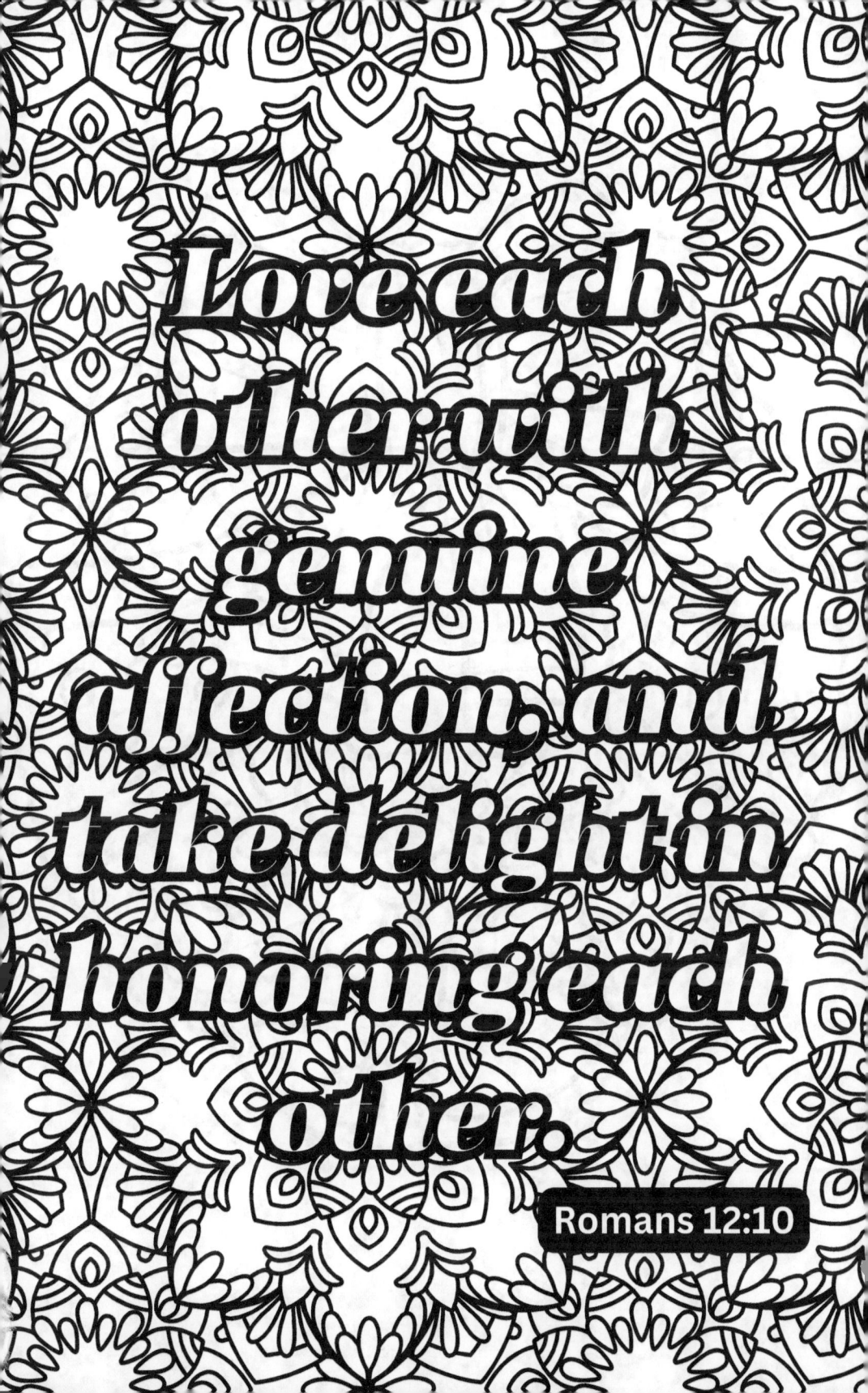

Love each other with genuine affection, and take delight in honoring each other.

Romans 12:10

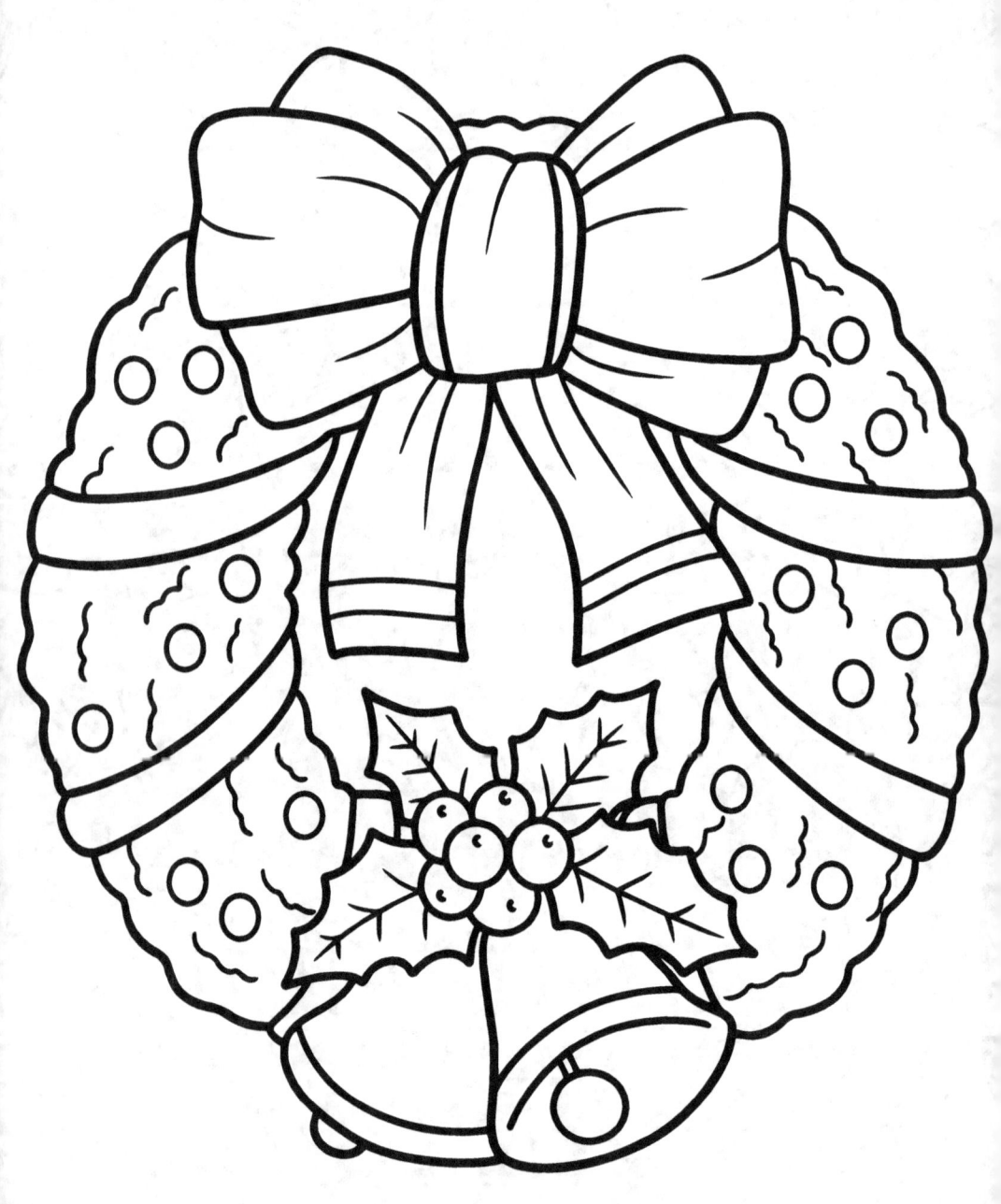

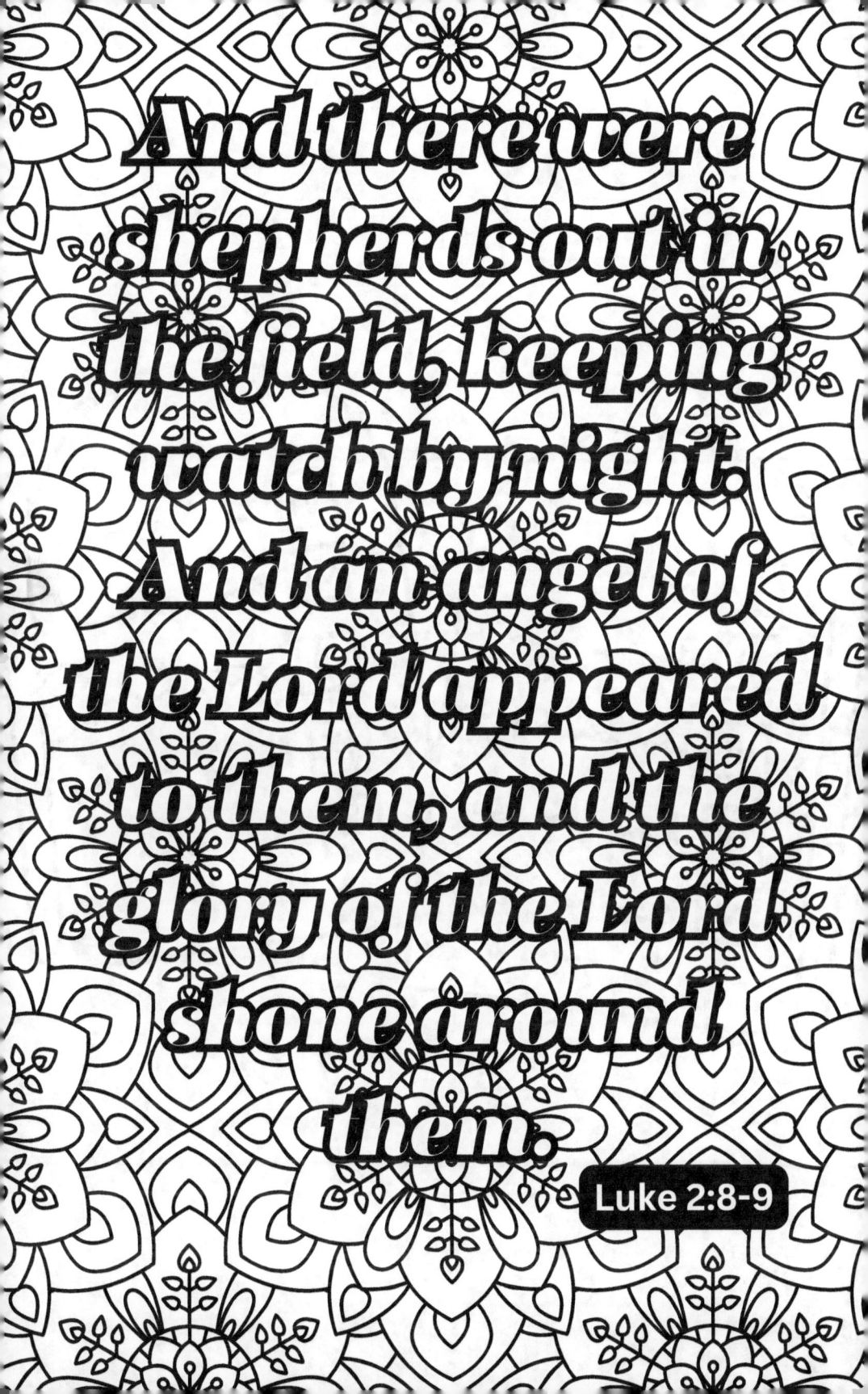

And there were shepherds out in the field, keeping watch by night. And an angel of the Lord appeared to them, and the glory of the Lord shone around them.

Luke 2:8-9

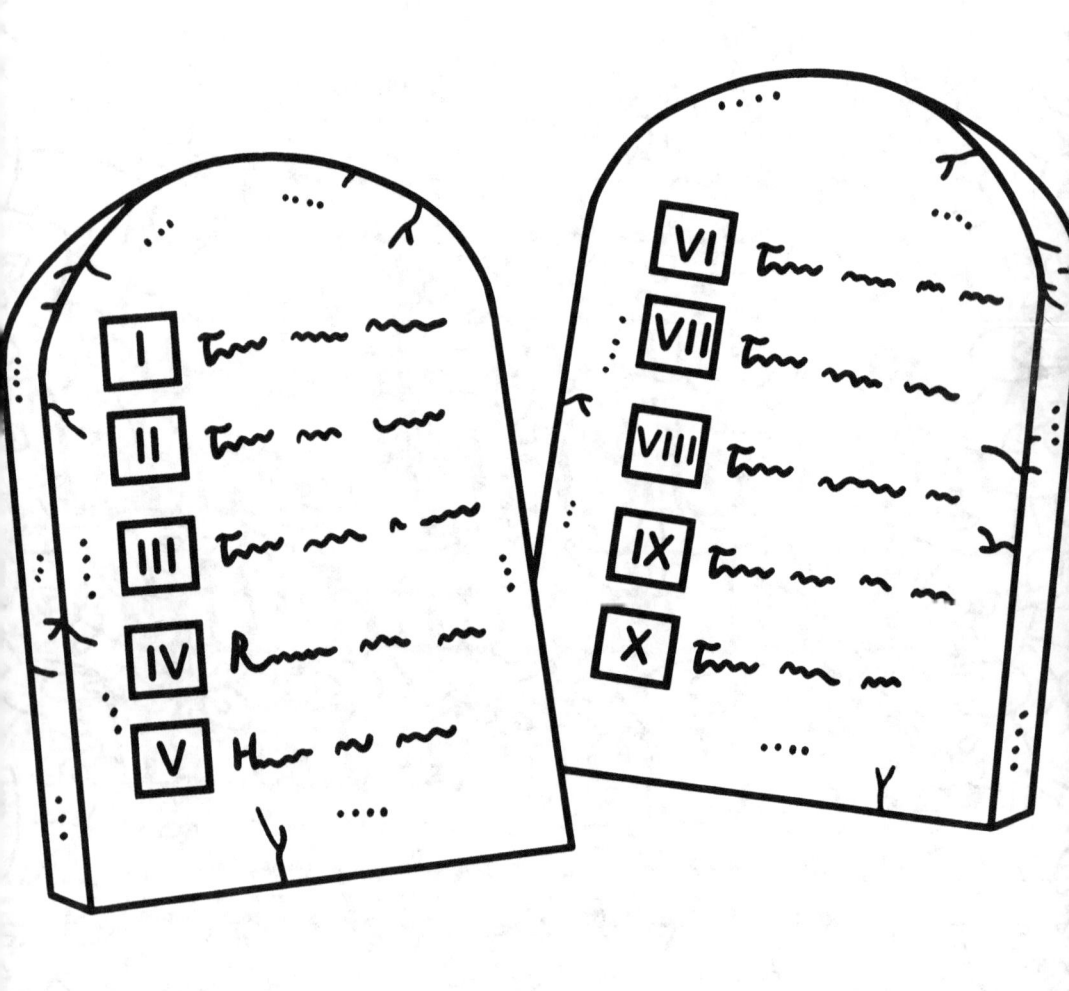

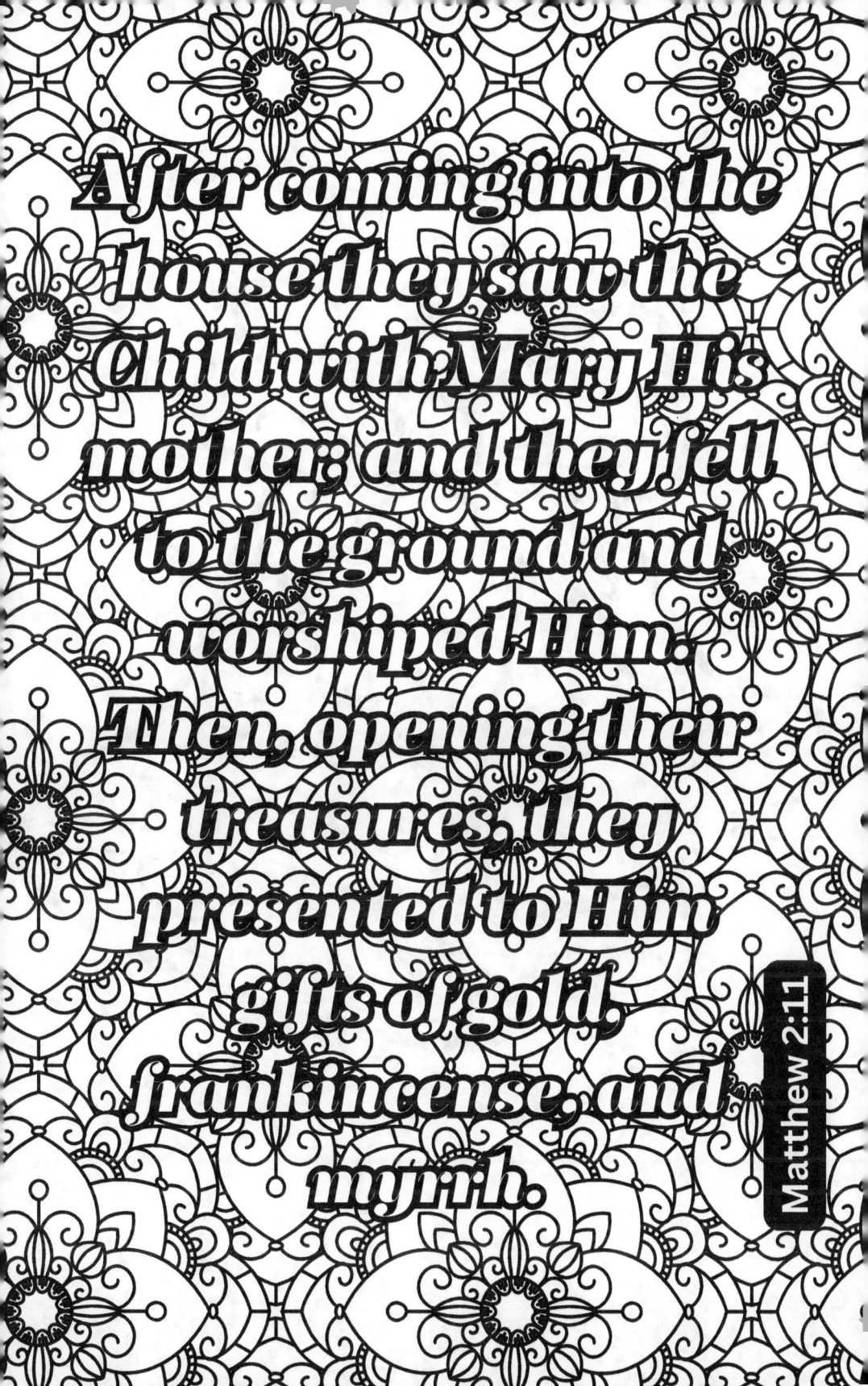

After coming into the house they saw the Child with Mary His mother; and they fell to the ground and worshiped Him. Then, opening their treasures, they presented to Him gifts of gold, frankincense, and myrrh.

Matthew 2:11

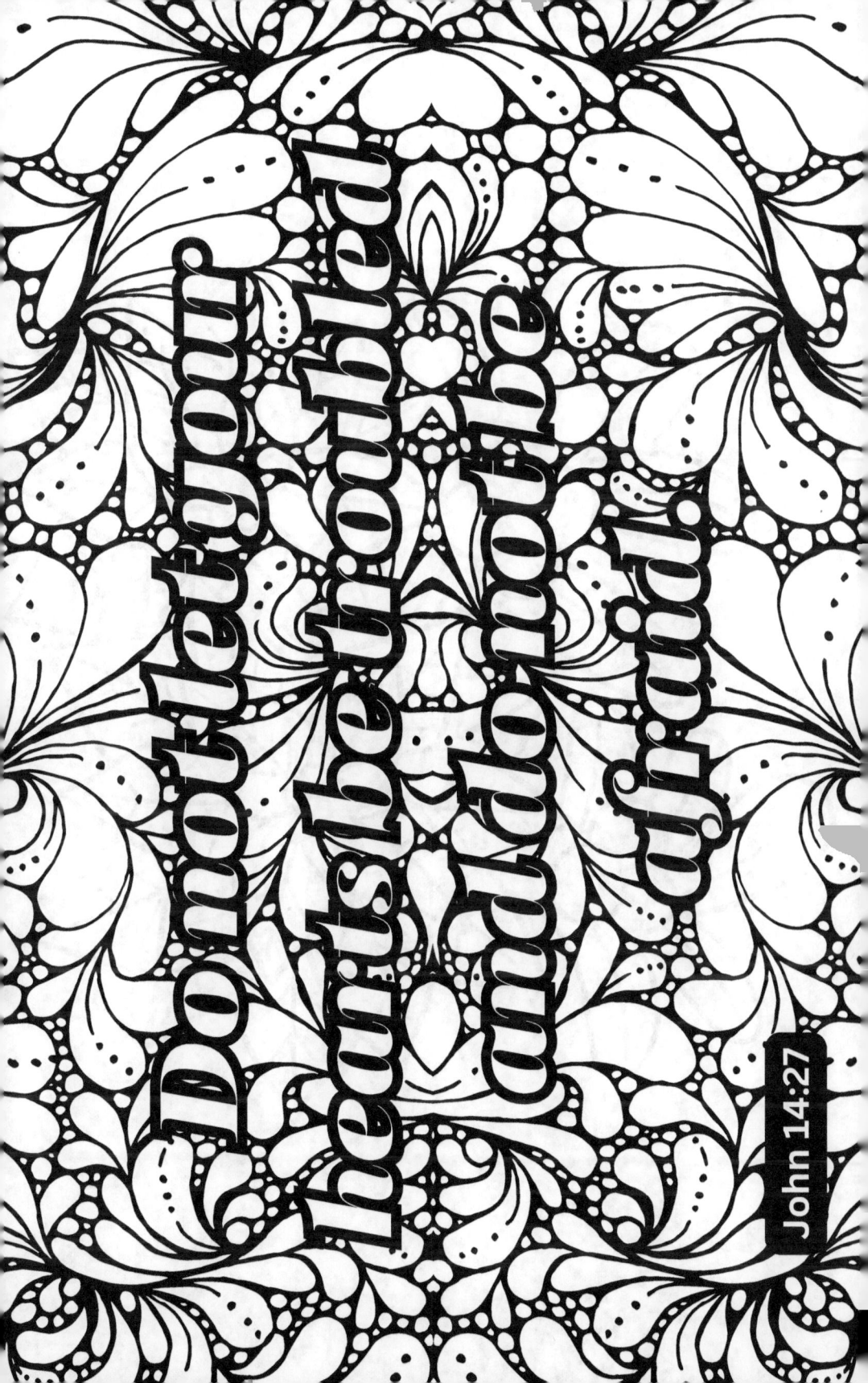

Do not let your
hearts be troubled
and do not be
afraid.

John 14:27

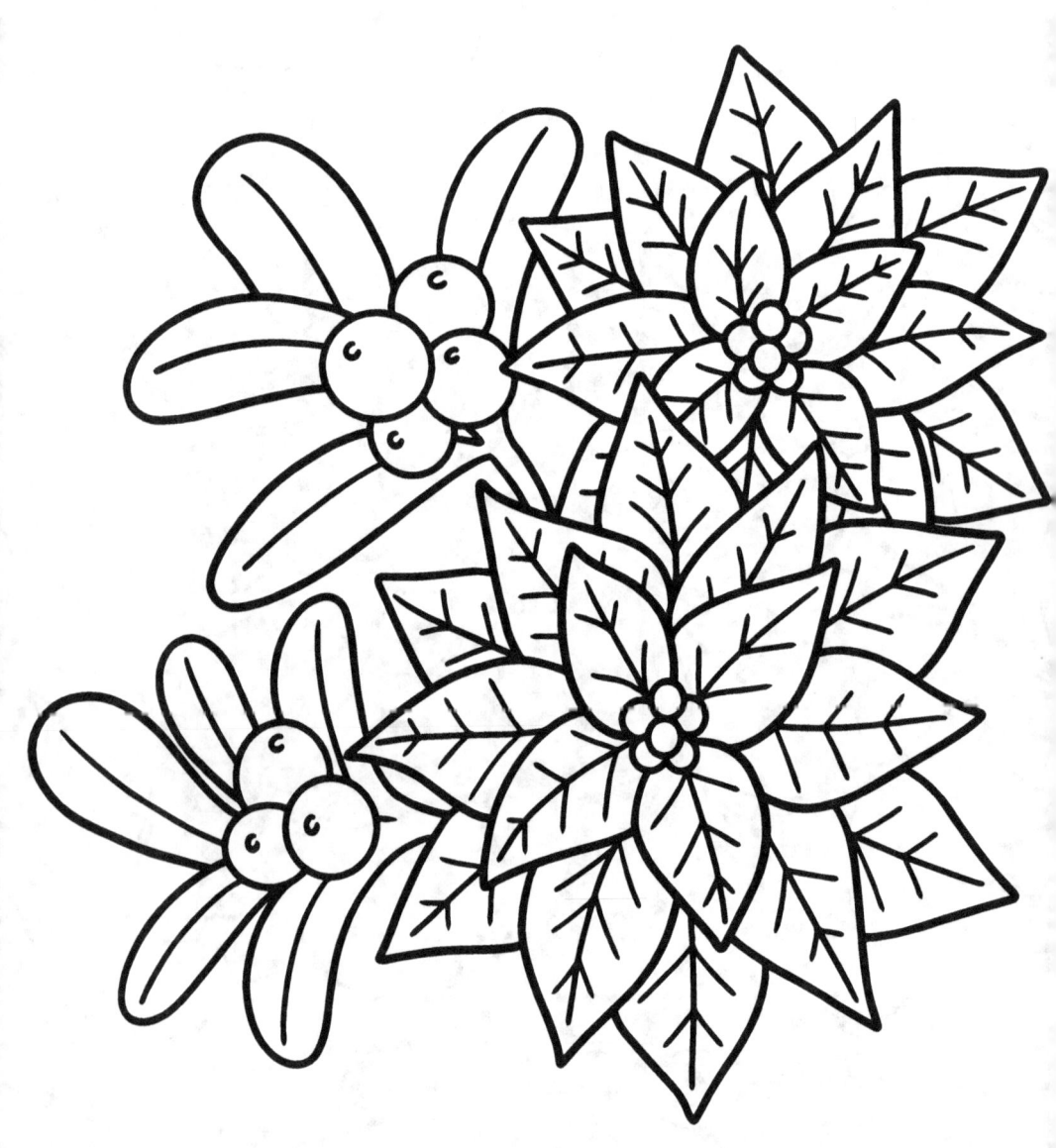

Peace I leave with you; my peace I give you. . . . I do not give to you as the world gives.

John 14:27

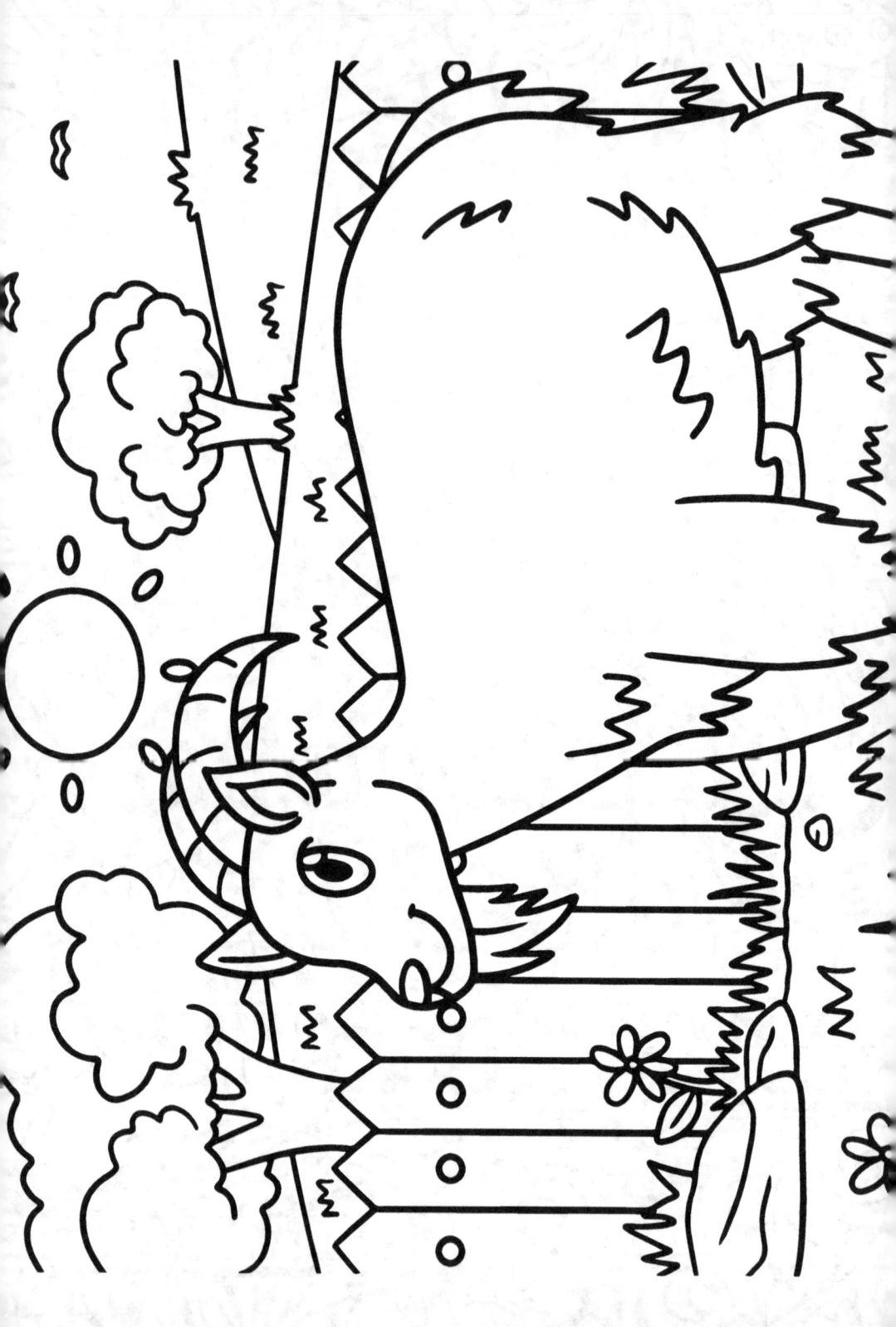

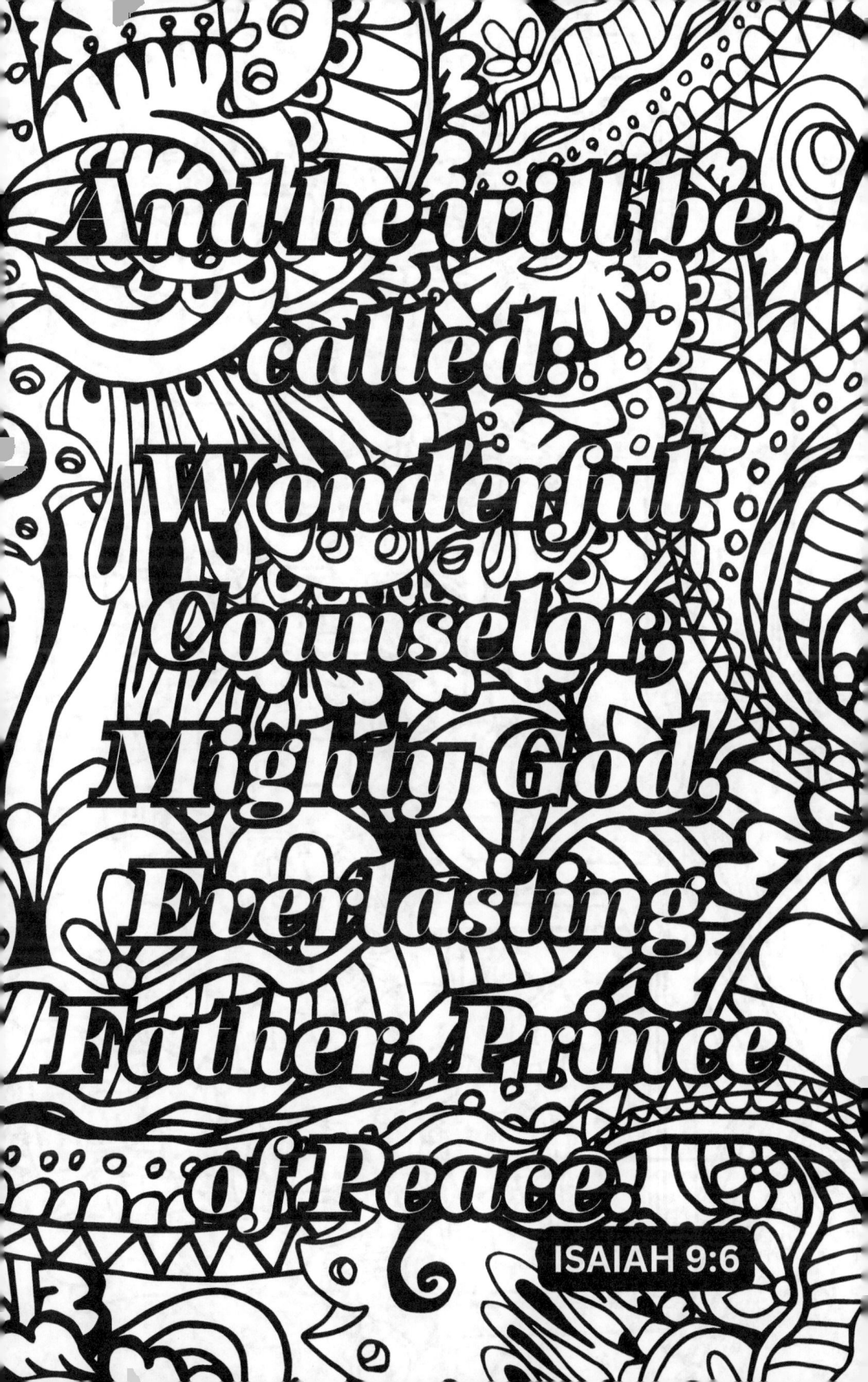

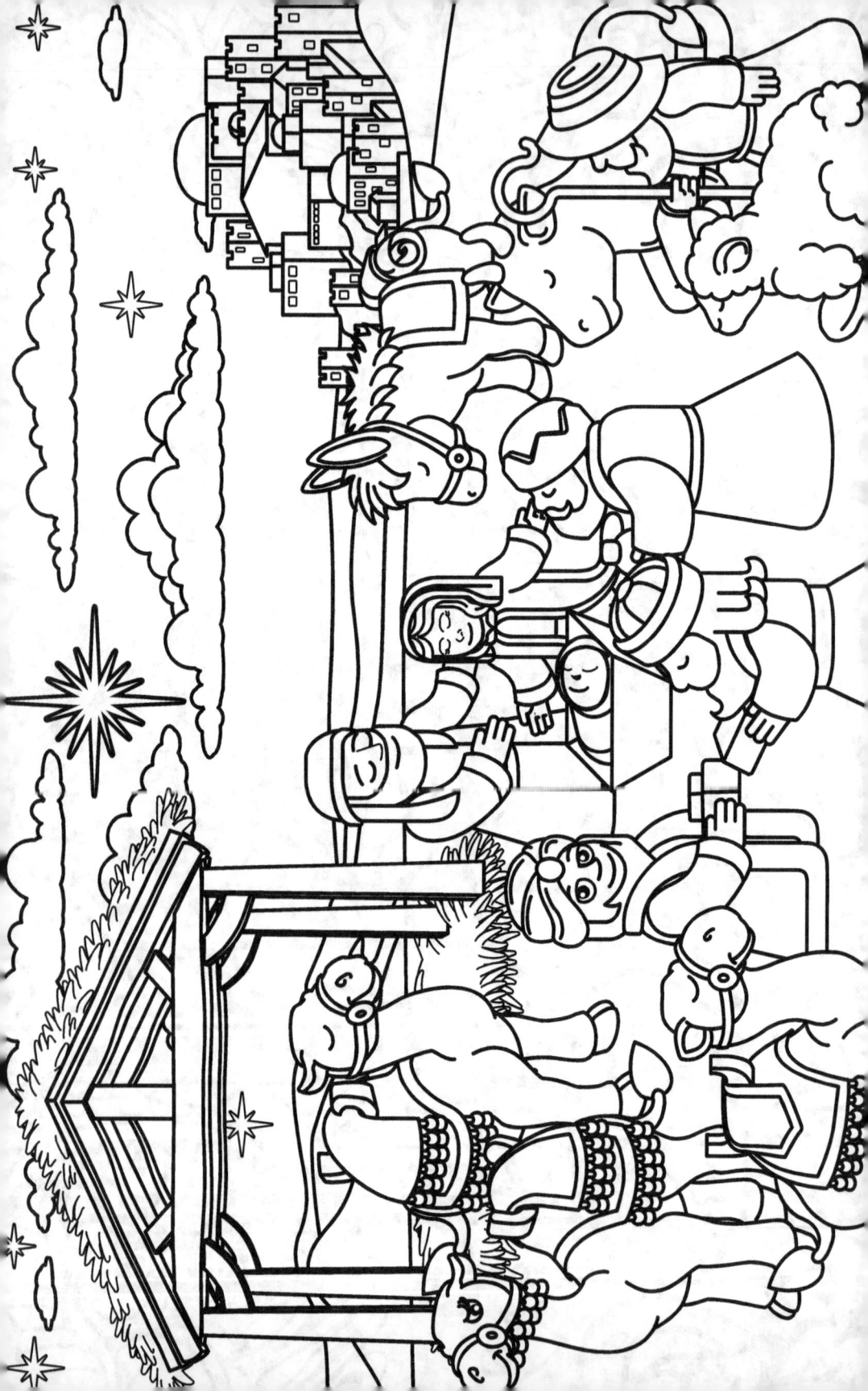

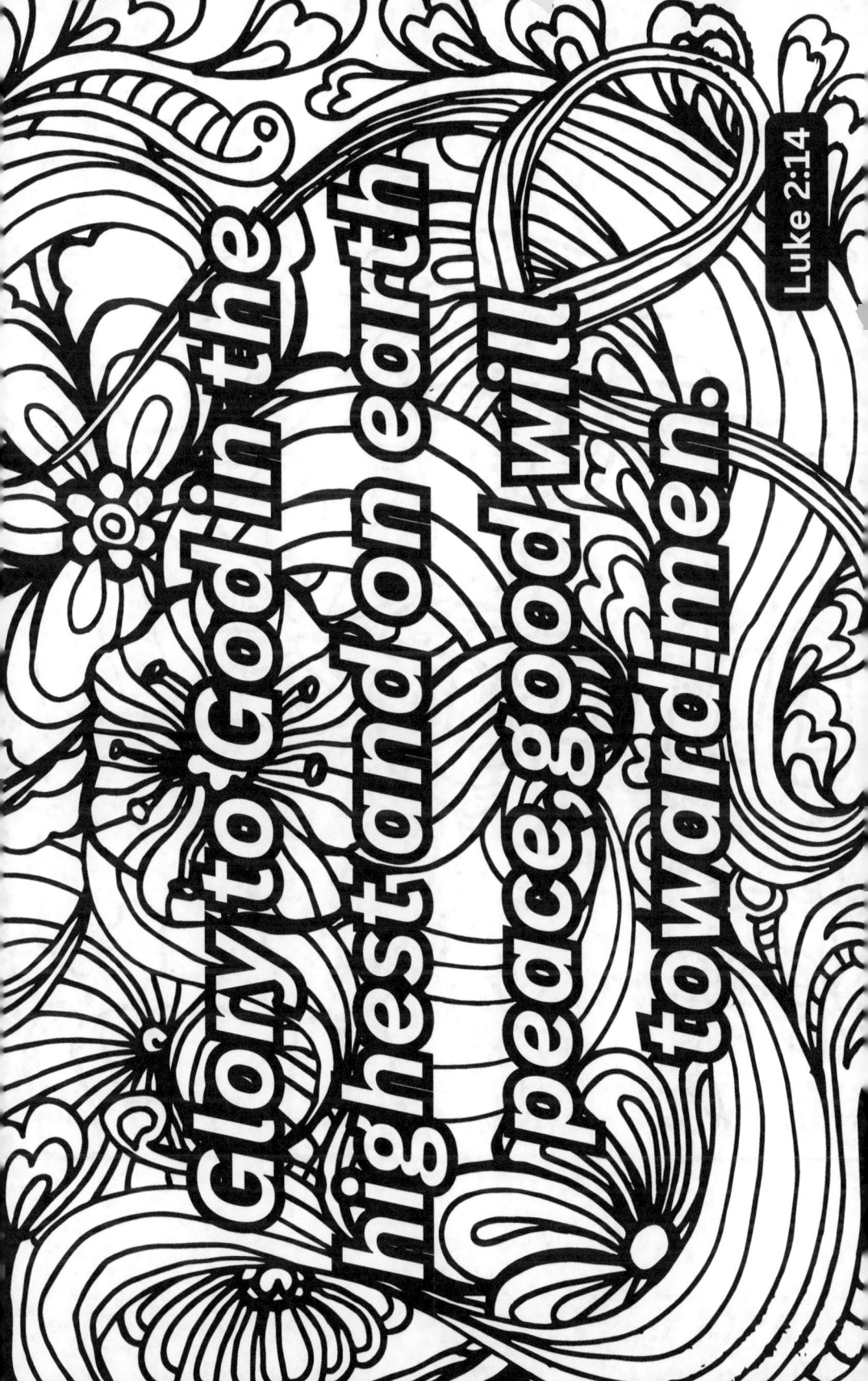

Luke 2:14

Glory to God in the highest and on earth peace, good will toward men.

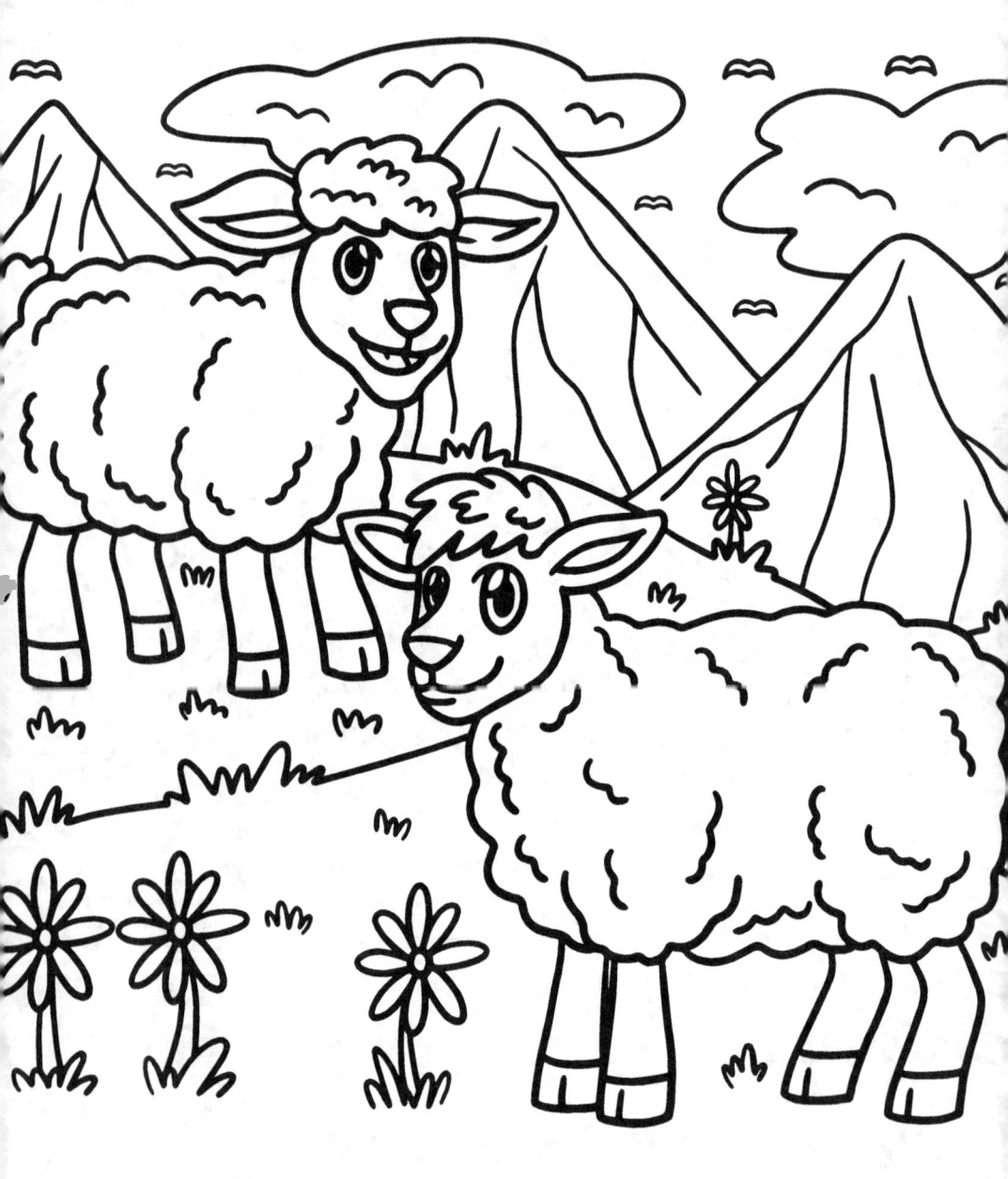

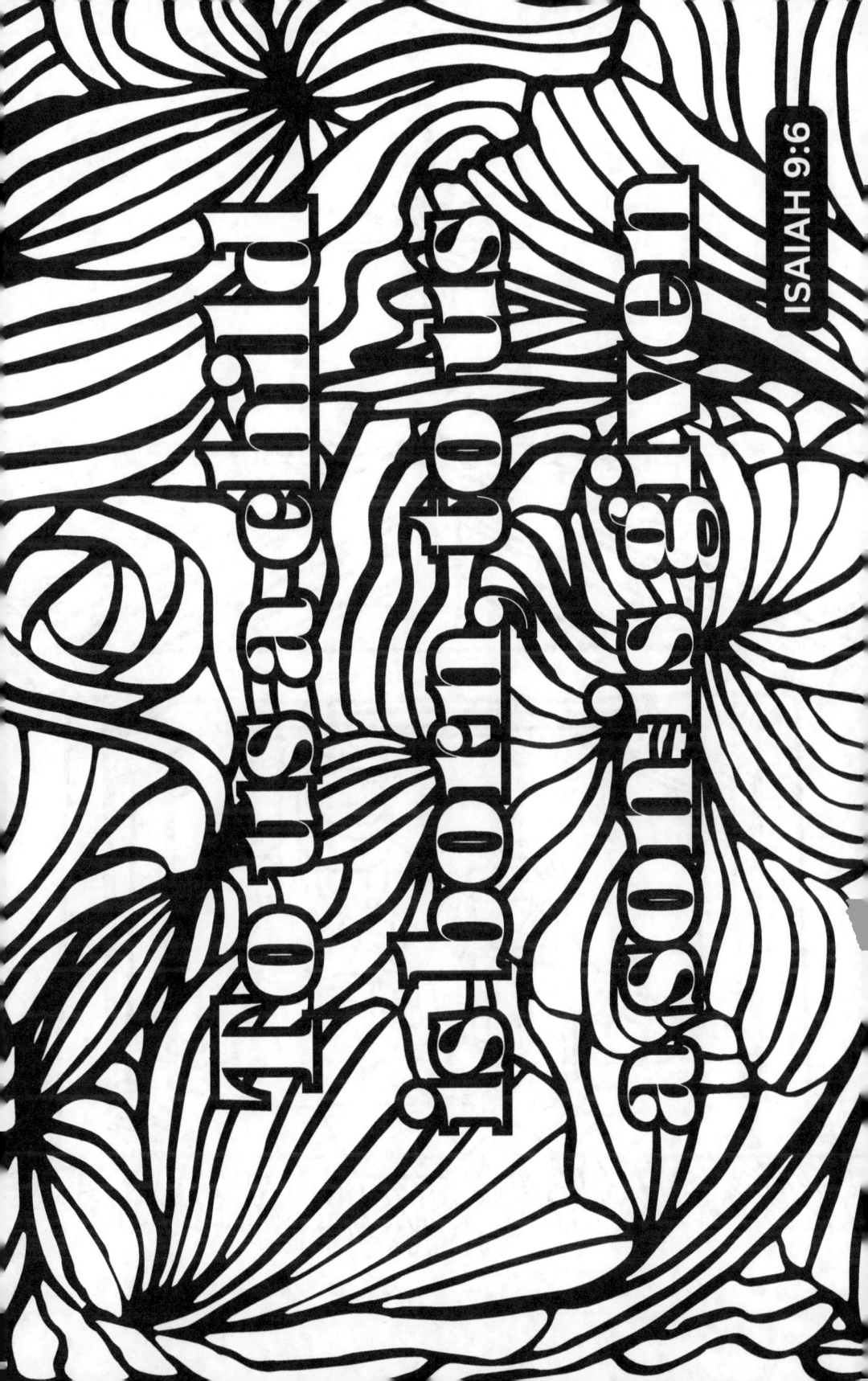

ISAIAH 9:6

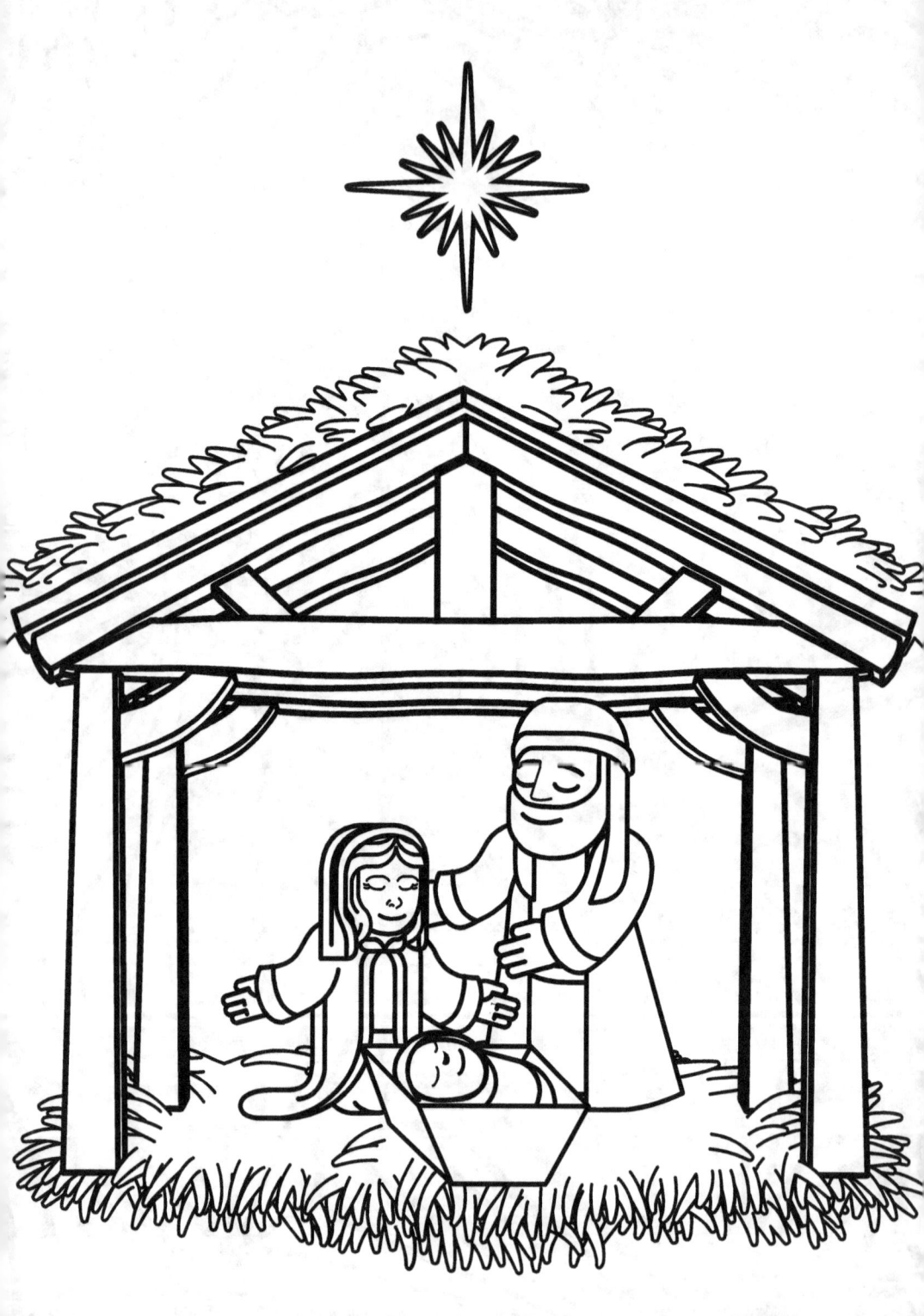

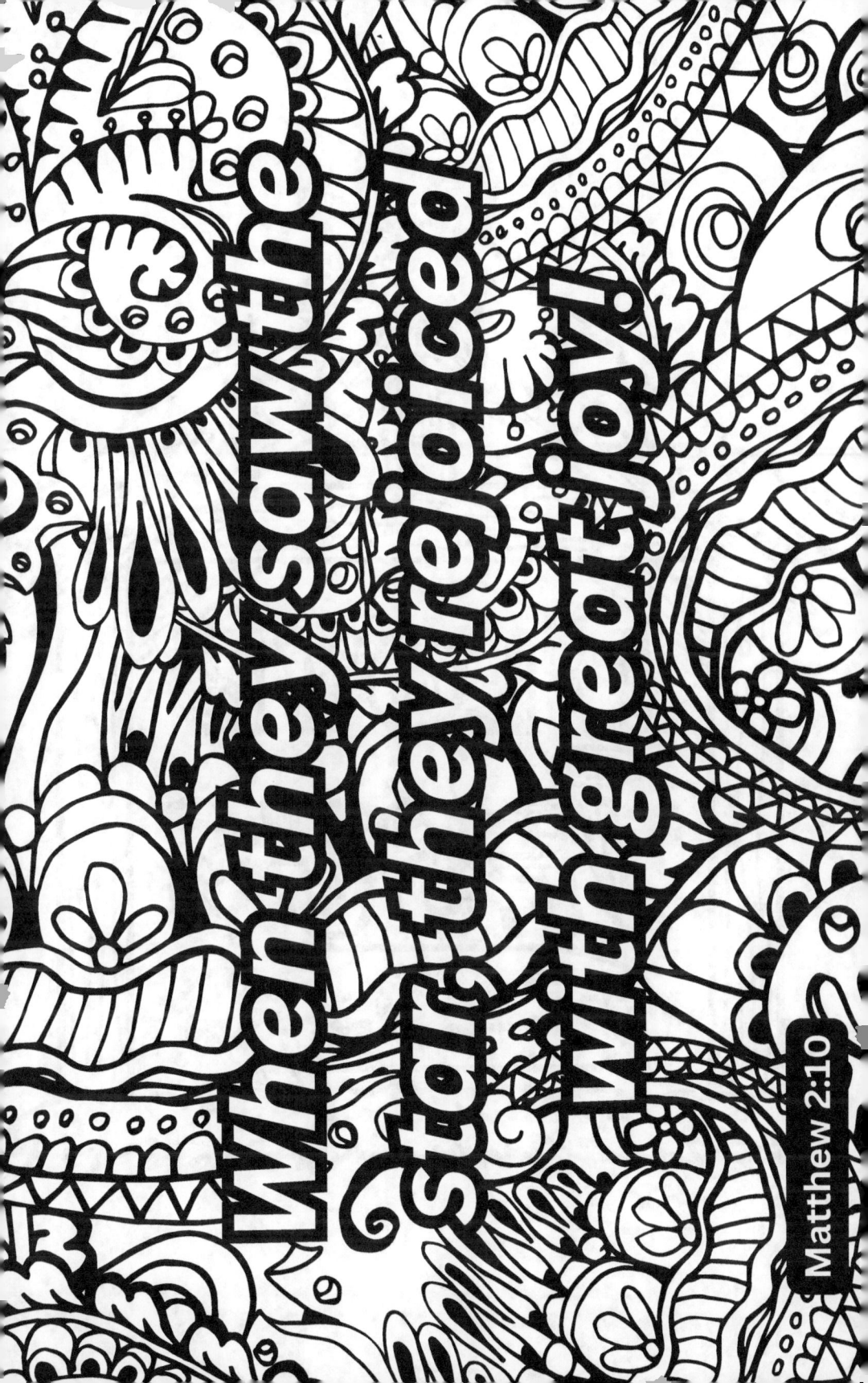

When they saw the star, they rejoiced with great joy!

Matthew 2:10

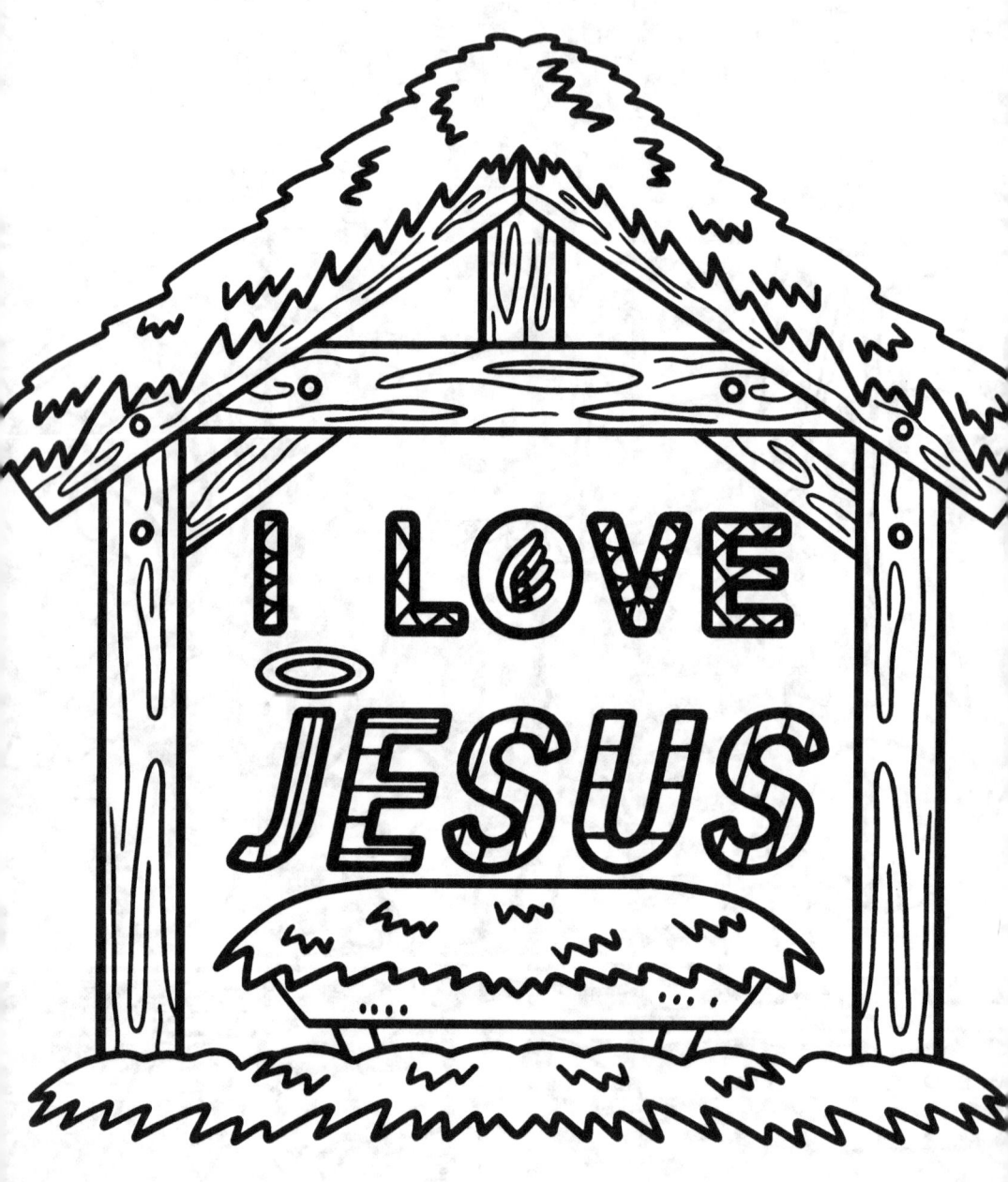

www.ingramcontent.com/pod-product-compliance
Lightning Source LLC
Chambersburg PA
CBHW072218290526
45794CB00007B/2788